Praise For

His Constant Call

In a world of noise that penetrates us from without and within, divine silence is the most vital spiritual praxis we must recover. Contemplation is the truest vocation of our humanity, yet we have largely forgotten the hidden Spring of Life, which is more experienced than taught. Nevertheless, there are "methodless methods" handed to us by the Great Tradition to assist our return to rest, fostering an awareness of our unity in the Trinitarian life. In this rich volume, Ken McCann helps reintroduce us to contemplative practice, offering valuable, accessible insights to help along the way.
— **John Crowder**

***

I've walked with Ken for 30 years or more. I know him intimately and know him to be a seeker and prayer warrior. This is a book that tells the reader in simple and doable terms how to grow in intimacy with God. Get it, read it, and do it. It will set you on a wonderful life path.
— **Jack Johnson**

***

I have loved reading Ken McCann's book *His Constant Call*, A Primer on Contemplative Prayer. His goal is not to elevate his own spiritual standing or set himself apart, but his goal is clearly to make contemplative prayer and a deeper relationship with the Lord something we all can grow in. Ken's experience, humble obedience, and ever-growing relationship with the Lord make him the perfect guide to those new to contemplative prayer, those frustrated in their path and those who have enjoyed a life full of talking to and listening to the Lord's voice. As someone who has practiced this type of prayer for many years with varying degrees of success, this book was a good reminder of where I started and where I'm still headed and mostly that God has faithfully walked with me all along the way. This book is an invitation; it is Ken's light put on its stand, giving light to us all, pointing us and guiding us to the ancient path.

—**Sarah C. Johnson**

***

Ken McCann's *His Constant Call* helped me make sense of my earliest religious addiction—listening for God's still, small voice. Ken's humble approach explains the why and how behind the potent spiritual discipline of prayer that will forever change how you relate to the Lord. Ken's words encourage new believers looking for a less formulaic encounter with Jesus and inspire those who are walking with Christ to ditch complicated, cumbersome strategies to approach the throne of grace with renewed curiosity and wonder.

— **Amy Denney**

HIS CONSTANT CALL

A Primer on Contemplative Prayer

Ken McCann

Published by KHARIS PUBLISHING, an imprint of KHARIS MEDIA LLC.

Copyright © 2025 Ken McCann

ISBN-13: 978-1-63746-558-5

ISBN-10: 1-63746-558-0

Library of Congress Control Number:

All rights reserved. This book or parts thereof may not be reproduced in any form, stored in a retrieval system, or transmitted in any form by any means - electronic, mechanical, photocopy, recording, or otherwise - without prior written permission of the publisher, except as provided by United States of America copyright law.

All scripture quotations, unless otherwise indicated, are from the New King James version, Copyright 1982 by Thomas Nelson, all rights reserved.

Scripture quotations marked AMP are from the Amplified Bible, copyright 2015 by The Lockman Foundation, La Habra, CA.

Scripture quotations marked ESV are from the English Standard Version, copyright 2001 by Crossway, a publishing ministry of Good News Publishers.

Scripture quotations marked NIV are from the New International Version, copyright 1973, 1978, 1984, 2011 by Biblica, Inc.

All KHARIS PUBLISHING products are available at special quantity discounts for bulk purchases for sales promotions, premiums, fund-raising, and educational needs. For details, contact:

Kharis Media LLC

Tel: +1 (331) 312-2376

support@kharispublishing.com

www.kharispublishing.com

*To Jack, Brian, and the Vineyard Christian Church,
Springfield, IL, present and past.*

My heartfelt gratitude and appreciation to Julie, Angela, Elaine, and Marek. Your wisdom, insight, patience, and gracious encouragement made this project a joy. Thank you!

To my wife and fellow sojourner of 40 years, Kelly. The countless hours of conversations defining and clarifying this wonderful path, and searching the heart of our God, have forever changed me. Thank you for creating this with me.

Table of Contents

Foreword xi

Introduction xiii

Chapter 1 A Place to Start 1

Chapter 2 Contemplative Prayer and Meditation 17

Chapter 3 The Ancient Paths of Contemplative Prayer 33

Chapter 4 The Secret Place, Solitude, and Interior Silence 53

Chapter 5 Search My Heart, Oh God 71

Chapter 6 Postures of the Heart 81

Chapter 7 Nurturing a Prayer Life: Some Practical Considerations 95

Chapter 8 A Long Obedience in the Same Direction 111

Chapter 9 Community 123

Chapter 10 Growing in Compassion 135

Epilogue 145

References 149

Foreword

I have always believed the Church/church to be a countercultural presence in the world. And just as life began to move faster, get noisier, and way more complicated, we began a journey to "be still and know." At times, it felt like slowly turning a large cruise ship away from the amusements of travel, sightseeing, and consuming all the things, towards an open sea.

This book captures the many elements of finding a better way. We had to dig up the mystics, the early church fathers and mothers, and the occasional contemporary mystic as we began to take an odd direction: into quiet, stillness, and prayer. Shh… Stop … Wait … As far as our church's agenda was concerned, less became more. And it was a place where many did not want to go.

But slowly, over time, a faithful few began to recognize the value of taking a different path. They discovered that spending 60 minutes a day going against the rising tide, resisting the overwhelming urge for more, more talk, more services, more possessions, more money, more choices, did in fact, promote peace and clarity. There was a quieting that came, a rest from all the machinations of the world.

His Constant Call is an invitation to an encounter. It is a book that may take you where something forever shifts and your life with God infiltrates your life on earth in simple and pleasant yet powerful ways, to a less-is-more kind of life.

It will require something of you, but it will be worth it.

Julie J

The Pastor's Wife

Introduction

And when you pray, you shall not be like the hypocrites. For they love to pray standing in the synagogues and on the corners of the streets, that they may be seen by men. Assuredly, I say to you, they have their reward. But you, when you pray, go into your room, and when you have shut your door, pray to your Father who is in the secret place; and your Father who sees in secret will reward you openly. And when you pray, do not use vain repetitions as the heathen do. For they think that they will be heard for their many words. **(Matthew 6:5-7)**

More than 20 years ago, my small, local church began a journey down the path of contemplative prayer as together we committed to spend at least an hour a day in prayer with Jesus. Led by our pastor and desiring to experience the fullness of Christ, we were challenged to make our relationship with Jesus at least as important as everything else in our lives. Of course, we agreed with this very reasonable request since He is the Lord and Savior. Our lives are His, right? Most Christians would agree. However, when this request became a requirement to spend at least an hour per day in prayer to remain engaged in our church community, it became apparent that this was no small thing. Our pastor simply required that each of us needed to assume responsibility for our relationship with our Lord so that he was able to pastor us in a way he felt led. We needed to grow up and learn to hear God for ourselves. Some members felt this was legalistic and chose to leave. For those of us who remained, our journey into contemplative prayer began, in part, motivated by the verse from Matthew's gospel above. We very quickly discovered the challenges of walking this out in our day-to-day lives.

The hour-per-day requirement provided a starting point – enough time from each day to require a reassessment and realignment of priorities in our busy lives. While it was never about adhering to an hour per day exactly, it did result in the realization that we struggled to sit still before our Lord for any length of time. Why was this so difficult? We were confronted with messy interior lives, our own rampant thoughts, and our inability to still and quiet our minds and souls. We were realizing this was the primary battleground for the renewing of our minds as Paul exhorts us in Romans 12:2:

> And do not be conformed to this world, but be transformed by the renewing of your mind, that you may prove what is that good and acceptable and perfect will of God.

Contemplative prayer was the model we would practice during this time with Him. As we began to sit before God in silence and solitude and present our hearts to Him, we began to understand this was more about time spent with Him, for Him, than time for us to bring Him our requests. A deep longing in our hearts to just 'be' in His presence was awakening within us.

We immersed ourselves in many helpful books and learned practical steps to set aside time. Challenges, victories, and failures were shared as a community, and we were encouraged and exhorted (and sometimes

His Constant Call

corrected) weekly by our pastor. The beautiful reality of contemplative prayer and the contemplative life soon emerged by the grace of God, with an emphasis on grace! It's taken time, lots of time, but we are learning to sit in quiet and stillness, with mouths closed and hearts open. We do it imperfectly, but our commitment is steadfast and our hearts are determined.

In the beginning, changes in my life resulting from contemplative prayer were often difficult to recognize. My world, however, was slowly being decompartmentalized. I began to converse with Jesus, expecting to notice the Holy Spirit's hand at work throughout the day, not just during my prayer time or church services. Beauty and wonder at life began to re-emerge as if my eyes had been reopened or readjusted. His faithfulness in all arenas of life became more visible, and my history with Him was developing a firm foundation, encouraging me that I could trust Him. This Christian journey, after all, is really about trust. What began as a discipline of setting time aside every morning eventually, after months and years, became a 'want to' and finally the most exciting and important time of every day that I no longer want to live without.

The challenges have been many, and the failures even more numerous, but success is not defined by how much time we spend or even how we spend our time with the Lord. Success is defined by a deepening relationship with our Savior and a growing confidence in His love and grace.

This primer has been written as an invitation to this path. It is based on our church community's experiences and includes quotes and references to the many books and resources that have encouraged us along this path. My prayer is that you will also experience deepening communion with Jesus as you respond to His constant call.

Chapter 1

A Place to Start

The whole outlook of mankind might be changed if we could all believe that we dwell under a friendly sky and that the God of heaven, though exalted in power and majesty, is eager to be friends with us.[1]

What are we doing?

In Psalm 27:4, David says,

> One thing I have desired of the Lord, that will I seek; that I may dwell in the house of the Lord all the days of my life, to behold the beauty of the Lord, and to inquire in his temple.

What is the 'one thing' that you desire? If, like David, it is to deepen your relationship and dwell with the Lord all the days of your life, you may find this primer on contemplative prayer helpful. Jesus promised His disciples that,

> If anyone loves Me, he will keep My word; and My Father will love him, and We will come to

---

[1] A.W Tozer, *Knowledge of the Holy* (New York: HarperCollins, 1961), pg. 83

> him and make Our home with him. **(John 14:23)**

David's cry focused on a physical temple, but the new covenant promises that we are the temple and the Godhead dwells within us! What a stunning reality! And yet, we struggle to prioritize our relationship with the Holy Trinity[2] and make a place for God in our busy lives. This should be the primary life-vision of every believer.

Making this a reality in our day-to-day lives is, unfortunately, not as simple as just responding to that mysterious longing deep inside of us to know Him more. While a response is absolutely required to begin this journey, we must overcome a number of obstacles and address paradoxes to make room for Him in our lives. As we learn to sit with Him in silence, we are simultaneously developing and deepening our conversational prayer life - that is, learning that we can communicate with our Lord anytime, anyplace, and in many different ways.

This walk with God is dependent upon and guided by His grace. Paradoxically, it requires that we implement disciplines in our lives that help us make room for Him. If we are not purposeful and tenacious about making this relationship a priority by setting aside time every day, it just will not happen. As our pastor used to say, "If you want to learn to pray everywhere all the time, you have to start to pray somewhere, some of the time." We will fail often. At times our lives seem

---

[2] Holy Trinity – refers to the triune God of the Christian Bible: Father, Son (Jesus), and Holy Spirit

overwhelming and out of control, but pursuing '*a long obedience in the same direction*'[3] does bear fruit. He is not disappointed in our failure and will continually draw us into a deeper relationship with Himself.

Why contemplative prayer?

Prayer has many connotations, and we likely have different definitions based on our experiences. For some of us, prayer means reciting ancient poems and creeds that may have lost their meaning for us. For others, presenting our laundry list of wants and needs is followed by a struggle to exercise faith so the Creator will deliver. Many of us conjure an image of sheepishly presenting our petitions to a scary God who seems impatient and irritated with us. We stand before him, praying he won't smite us! Hopefully, this primer will help redefine prayer as an opportunity for a deep relationship with a God Who desires to be with us.

In *Secrets of the Secret Place*, author Bob Sorge says,

> Prayer, in the true biblical sense, is the full spectrum of human expressions to God. Prayer is the all-encompassing title to describe the entire gamut of expressions we offer up to God.[4]

I wholeheartedly agree with Sorge that our expressions towards our Creator are quite limitless. Vocalizing

---

[3] Friedrich Nietzsche, "*Beyond Good and Evil*" in *A Long Obedience in the Same Direction* by Eugene Peterson (Downers Grove: InterVarsity Press, 2000) pg. 13.

[4] Bob Sorge, *Secrets of the Secret Place* (Grandview: Oasis House, 2018), pg. 81

requests and silently offering adoration to God are just a couple of common types of prayer.

Contemplative prayer presents a model of prayer that includes the disciplines of silence and solitude. Not to be confused with eastern religious definitions of contemplation that seek silence and solitude to clear one's consciousness, Christian contemplation is focused on spending time alone *with our Savior* to allow the Holy Spirit to reveal us to ourselves as He reveals Himself to us. It is during this quiet time alone with Him that He can access deep areas of our heart and reveal His purposes for us. While contemplation is not the only form of prayer, I believe this type of prayer is critical for us to be '*conformed to the image of His Son.*'[5]

How we hold our hearts as we approach Him is key to experiencing all He has for us. After all, He is Creator and we are the created, and it seems to me that we should at some point be compelled to simply sit before Jesus in humility, alone and in silence. To just 'be' in His presence as the ultimate posture of faith in His heart for us. While this may be the most challenging posture of the human heart – to remain still and quiet before Him - I believe He draws every believer to this place at some point in our journey. This is the place of contemplative prayer. Here is where we are confronted with the truth about ourselves and learn that we can trust that Jesus really does work all things for good in our lives. We cannot get there on our own, but His grace is sufficient and available as we persevere in our pursuit of a deeper relationship with Him. In the pages

---

[5] Romans 8:29

that follow, we will discuss challenges we face along with practical guidance to help us on this journey.

The long history of individuals who have practiced, taught, and written about contemplative prayer for centuries offers valuable instruction and encouragement. Those who have gone before also provide a wealth of language to describe the mysteries and experiences of prayer.

While the centuries of written guidance and documented experiences have been invaluable on this journey and continue to be a source of encouragement and guidance, we also recognize that no one person has the ultimate truth regarding a relationship with God. As Paul instructs the believers in Corinth:

> For now, we see in a mirror, dimly, but then face to face. Now I know in part, but then I shall know just as I am also known.
> **(1 Corinthians 13:12)**

There is no right way to participate in this relationship. The only wrong way is not to do it!

Growing in what we already have

Before we begin to discuss contemplative prayer as a way to seek our Lord, we must try to clarify what we are pursuing as we reprioritize our time and energy. We are not trying to earn anything, such as His gaze or affection, but we are striving to make a place for Him in our busy lives. This is the battleground in our postmodern, harried lives, and an hour per day is a great place to start. If that seems too much to sacrifice, consider the time we spend watching TV, at sporting events, or on our phones or computers. The choice and prioritization of our time is ours alone. As we choose to spend time pursuing this relationship, the Holy Spirit will unlock a deep longing in our hearts as He told Jeremiah:

> Then [with a deep longing] you will seek Me and require Me [as a vital necessity] and [you will] find Me when you search for Me with all your heart. I will be found by you, says the Lord. **(Jeremiah 29:13-14 AMP)**

We fail often and begin again, but He will be found by us as He promises! It is our heart's response to Him that moves His heart to draw us into a deeper relationship.

We must be clear, however, that as believers we have already received the fullness of Christ, as Paul wrote to the Colossians:

> For in Him dwells all the fullness of the Godhead bodily; and you are complete in Him, who is the head of all principality and power. **(Colossians 2:9-10)**

We are maturing in the knowledge and understanding of what He has already accomplished in us. As John Crowder states in *Mystical Union*,

> We completely affirm Christian growth. Even Jesus grew in wisdom and favor. We grow in lots of things. We are going from glory to glory. From light to light – for in His light we see light (Ps. 36:9). The expression of His faith is always growing in us. And primarily, we are growing in the renewal of the mind. What does that mean, to have the mind renewed? It is being

> continually awakened to the truth of what Christ has already accomplished. It is being renewed to something. And that "something" is a Reality that has already arrived.[6]

Contemplative prayer is a posture of our hearts, along with a commitment to make this relationship a priority in order to experience more fully what Jesus purchased for us and has placed within us. The moment we accepted Jesus as our Lord and Savior, the fullness of the Godhead came to dwell within us. As Crowder puts it,

> Your union with God in Christ is instant and effortless. It happened on the cross and was realized the first moment you believed. It is from this vantage point of being "in Christ" that all other doctrines of the church must be built.[7]

Crowder goes on to say,

> [We are] constantly growing in a greater and greater revelation of His fullness. But it is a fullness we already have. In fact, God was never impressed with your seeking to begin with. He was impressed with *His Son* who searched you out. You did not choose Him; He chose you (John 15:16). You will never be able

---

[6] John Crowder, *Mystical Union* (Marylhurst: Sons of Thunder Ministries and Publications, 2016) pg. 83
[7] Ibid, pg. 23

> to boast in your own ability to *choose* the Lord or seek Him out – you can only thank Him.[8]

This is such an important point! It is worth repeating that contemplative prayer, or the practice of any spiritual discipline, doesn't earn us anything. Rather, they are steps we take to allow the Holy Spirit to awaken the reality of what is already inside of us.

What we think about God is important

What we believe about God is critical to the health of our spiritual journey. We all have ideas about God that are incorrect and incomplete. There are many scriptural truths about His heart for us, but some of us are unavailable to receive these truths. For example, the basic truth that He is for us and desires to be in communion with us is foreign to many of us. I agree with A.W. Tozer's statement in *Knowledge of the Holy*, "What comes into our minds when we think about God is the most important thing about us."[9] Hugh Halter adds from his book *Sacrilege*,

> Here is a truth that affects us all: what you believe about Jesus is the most important influence in your life. You see, our beliefs affect our attitudes, our attitudes affect our behaviors, and our behaviors determine our future. Prov. 23:7 says, "*For as he thinks in his heart, so is he.*"[10]

We are a compilation of our experiences, decisions, observations, education, and unique way of processing

---

[8] John Crowder, *Mystical Union*, pg. 118
[9] A.W. Tozer, *Knowledge of the Holy*, pg. 1
[10] Hugh Halter, *Sacrilege* (Grand Rapids: Baker Books, 2011) pg. 24

information. Additionally, our giftings and unique personality from God impact how we perceive and process information around us. All of these influences impact our perceptions and opinions, and comprise our perspective or world view, through which all of the external input we receive is filtered into our hearts. These influences affect how we think and act. We must recognize that these influences also impact our thoughts about God; how we perceive Him and His relation to us. Additionally, even good and holy thoughts about God fall magnitudes short of who He really is, as our human minds are not capable of understanding or knowing Him, except what He has chosen to reveal to us. All of us have different impressions and ideas of who God is, and they are all inadequate at best and blatantly incorrect at worst. This sounds harsh, but we must recognize our perceptions, especially about God, need to be held before Him so He can realign them with Truth.

God's plan from the beginning was to dwell with man

We must settle in our hearts that He is for us and desires a relationship with us more than we desire Him. The whole library of scripture is a story about God's desire to be in relationship with His created humans. From the Garden of Eden to the New Jerusalem descending from the clouds, the Bible's primary message is the Lord's desire to be with us. As Michael Morales says in *Who Will Ascend God's Holy Mountain*,

> Life with God in the house of God – this was the original goal of the creation of the cosmos, and which then became the goal of redemption,

> the new creation. Entering the house of God to dwell with God, beholding, glorifying and enjoying him eternally, I suggest, is the story of the Bible, the plot that makes sense of the various acts, persons and places of its pages, the deepest context for its doctrines. For this ultimate end, the Son of God shed His blood and poured out the Spirit from on high, even to bring us into his Father's house, in him, as sons and daughters of God.[11]

Before the beginning of creation and time itself, He made a way to not only dwell with us but to dwell within us through the sacrifice of Jesus:

> …He chose us in Christ [actually selected us for Himself as His own] before the foundation of the world… In love He predestined and lovingly planned for us to be adopted to Himself as [His own] children through Jesus Christ, in accordance with the kind intention and good pleasure of His will… **(Ephesians 1:3-6 AMP)**

And

> Jesus answered and said to him, "If anyone loves Me, he will keep My word; and My Father will love him, and We will come to him and make Our home with him. **(John 14:23)**

Through Jesus, a way was made for God to dwell with man, in man, and eventually together as in the Garden

---

[11] Michael Morales, *Who Shall Ascend the Mountain of the Lord?* (Downers Grove: InterVarsity Press, 2015) pgs. 17& 21-22

of Eden. While these words seem to make sense in our minds, I believe the truth of this incredible revelation takes time to grow in our hearts. We are in good company, as scripture indicates it took the disciples, who lived with Jesus for 3 years, time to process this new paradigm of God's relationship with man.

Imagine how difficult it must have been for the disciples to receive Jesus' words at the Last Supper. For example, among many other things, He told them clearly that He and the Father were one.[12] He then told them that He and the Father would come to dwell in those who believe in Him.[13] He also told them the Spirit of Truth will be given to all who believe in Him.[14] Jesus knew these words challenged their understanding of God, and they would need time for this revelation to grow. He said, "*I still have many things to say to you, but you cannot bear them now*" (John 16:12). Would they have abandoned Jesus that night if they had understood all He said?

The God of their Hebrew Bible, our Old Testament, required the blood of blameless animals in order for Him to be near to humans. The Temple (or Tabernacle before that) was the only location on earth where YHWH met with humanity. And this occurred only once a year, as only the high priest could enter the Holy of Holies before His presence. This would have been one of the primary stories of the Hebrew Bible that the disciples were brought up with. They would have listened over and over to the words of the Hebrew

---

[12] John 14:9-11
[13] John 14:23
[14] John 14:16-17

Bible their entire lives. And now they were being told that those scriptures were being fulfilled by Jesus, but in a way they did not understand.

The point is that, like us, the disciples needed time to process this life-changing revelation that defies human logic and their Old Testament teachings. They needed patient instruction over the coming weeks and months (and years) to grasp the intense love of Jesus and the meaning of His death and resurrection. We see examples of the patient instruction of Jesus after His resurrection on the road to Emmaus, as Jesus opened their eyes and the scriptures to them concerning Himself.

> And beginning at Moses and all the Prophets, He expounded to them in all the Scriptures the things concerning Himself. **(Luke 24:27)**

Luke's gospel tells us this instruction continued. Jesus appeared as the disciples were together, listening to the two disciples share their encounter with Jesus on the road to Emmaus. Oh, to be there as He *opened their understanding, that they might comprehend the Scriptures*. (Luke 24:45) This is the same God who desires fellowship with us, and His patient instruction is as true for us as it was for them!

This essential revelation that His heart is for us and forever filled with intense love towards us is what will sustain us when we feel He is distant or has abandoned us. This, I believe, is the essence of the Christian Walk of faith.

What we believe about ourselves is equally important

While our sin nature was nailed to the cross with Jesus, along with the old man, our perspectives, based upon our experience, opinions, and perceptions, are not completely transformed when we are born again. We need new neuronal pathways forged and old/wrong ones destroyed as we grow in relationship with Jesus and the revelation of what He has done for us and placed within us. Not only do we need a revelation of His heart for us, but we simultaneously need a revelation of who we are in Him and the life He's given us once we accept Jesus as our Lord and Savior.

All of this – an immature or incorrect understanding of God's heart for us, together with an immature or incorrect understanding of who we are in Jesus – means we have limited capacity to fully experience the true reality of who He is. We get glimpses here and there, but as our relationship matures and deepens, He expands our ability to receive more of the revelation of His life within us. Additionally, an immature heart seeks its own validation and acceptance. Father Ronald Rolheiser writes in his book *The Shattered Lantern*,

> ...we ache for a cure for our mortality and insignificance and so we fabricate the vital lie. We try, through our own efforts, to create for ourselves significance, uniqueness, and immortality.[15]

---

[15] Ronald Rolheiser, *The Shattered Lantern* (New York: Crossroad Publishing Co., 2001) pg. 131

Instead of finding peace and rest in who we are in Jesus, we strive to define ourselves to the world around us.

God does not condemn our immaturity

It seems many of us are vulnerable to condemnation, comparison, judgment, and feelings of failure that can stifle our progress in this love relationship. Our inner dialogue sometimes tells us, "We can never do enough, consistently enough, to make Him happy." We give ear to these accusations because of our own perception of what this relationship should look like. While God corrects and redirects us, He does not condemn our weakness and immaturity the way we think He should, or the way we do to ourselves and others. I've found Mike Bickle's teachings on immaturity and how God sees us from his *Life of David* and *Song of Solomon* teaching series very helpful in understanding the Father's patience and acceptance of me, even in my immaturity. Letting these truths become part of our internal prayer dialogue and beliefs about Jesus will enable us to run to Him, not turn away from Him, even when we sin and fail. As Bickle says,

> "Our repentance, obedience and love for God are sincere even while they are weak and flawed. Weak love is not false love, therefore, Jesus values our love for Him even when it is weak."[16]

Let this truth sink into our hearts and encourage us that He delights in us even as we grow and mature in our relationship with Him. Sure, we must repent when we

---

[16] Mike Bickle, *The Song of Songs* (Kansas City: Forerunner Publishing, 2007) pg. 28

sin, as He does not turn a blind eye to sin in our lives. But neither does He disqualify us when we fall or sin, repent, and get up and walk again. As we see in the lives of the disciples, the pursuit of complete obedience takes time, perhaps a lifetime, but Jesus does not disqualify them because of their immaturity.

Peter, as an example

Peter is a favorite example of the patience of Jesus. This hard-headed fisherman thinks he has things figured out and falls time and again. His perceptions of who Jesus is and what He has come to do had to be deconstructed and realigned to the truth. Consider that Jesus washed the feet of Peter, whom He knew would deny Him. Most of us have no grid for how to apply this level of humility to our own lives. Jesus met Peter where he was in the moment, knowing what he would become as he matured in the truth of who Jesus is:

> "…Where I am going, you cannot follow Me now, but you shall follow Me afterwards." **(John 13:36)**

What a powerful example of Jesus's heart for us!

According to John's gospel, there were at least two meetings between Jesus and the disciples after the resurrection before Peter's denial was dealt with. We can only imagine how Peter may have struggled to look His resurrected Savior in the eye with the unresolved conflict of his denial in his heart. Why did Jesus wait to reinstate Peter? I suggest it's because He patiently waited for him to be prepared to receive what He had for him. Jesus also patiently waits for us. His timing is perfect.

His Constant Call

John's gospel tells us Peter and the others went fishing while waiting for further instruction from Jesus. This gives us a glimpse of Peter's conflicted heart as he returned to the life he knew before meeting Jesus. Out in the boat after an unsuccessful night of fishing, they didn't recognize Jesus on the shore. He instructed them to cast their nets on the right side of their boat, and they caught a multitude of fish. John then recognized Jesus:

> Then that disciple (John) whom Jesus loved said, "Peter, it is the Lord!" So when Simon Peter heard that it was the Lord, he put on his outer tunic and threw himself into the sea and swam ashore. **(John 21:7 AMP)**

Peter jumped off the boat when he realized that Jesus was the man on the shore! Something inside immediately drew him to Jesus. It seems likely that Peter had unresolved conflict in his heart from his denial. Did he wonder if the man he had denied would receive him as he swam to shore? And yet, when he got to shore, he ran to Him. This is so important! I can only imagine how his countenance may have fallen and courage left him when he got to shore, face-to-face with the man he had denied. But then it was too late – Jesus had him! He powerfully reinstated Peter. He called him forward from the mistakes of the past to walk into the future He had for him. We must learn not to delay in turning our hearts to Him after we fail! God delights in showing us mercy. He wants us to be confident that He enjoys us (even in our weakness) as we walk in sincere repentance.

Chapter 2

Contemplative Prayer and Meditation

The truly spiritual person, tradition teaches us knows that spirituality is concerned with how to live a full life, not an empty one. Real spirituality is life illumined by a compelling search for wholeness. It is contemplation at the eye of chaos. It is life lived to the full...Spirituality is about coming to consciousness of the sacred. It is in that consciousness that perspective comes, that peace comes. It is in that consciousness that a person comes to wholeness. Life is not an exercise to be endured. It is a mystery to be unfolded.[1]

Christ-centered spiritual activities

In this chapter, we will begin to define contemplative prayer and meditation. These activities go hand-in-hand and describe spiritual exercises or ways we interact with God. These terms are often confused with practices of other Eastern religions. It is important to clarify at the outset that we are discussing *Christian* contemplative prayer and meditation. The differences

---

[1] Joan Chittister, *Illuminated Life* (Maryknoll: Orbis Books, 2000) pgs. 13-14&16

with other religions may seem subtle, but they are very important. For example, we will discuss the importance of solitude, which means being alone. We believe, however, that we are never truly alone. Instead, we are meeting with our Lord and Savior. Additionally, we will discuss practices to help clear our minds and control our thoughts. Our goal is not to reach a state of thoughtless emptiness. Rather, we seek to set aside our preoccupation with ourselves in order to make room for the Holy Spirit. We give Him access to our inner life, our minds and souls, in ways that we are unable to recognize through our human senses. In other words, we are sitting alone before God, with God, and believe that He is communicating with our spirits at a depth we are not able to discern with our physical senses.

Contemplative prayer

The practice of contemplative prayer, or contemplation, is difficult to define concisely. Trappist Monk and contemplative, Thomas Merton, put it this way,

> For contemplation cannot be taught. It cannot even be clearly explained. It can only be hinted at, suggested, pointed to, or symbolized.[2]

It describes an intimate interaction with God that requires our entire being. As you read the following pages, I encourage you to please be patient with me (and yourself). I am trying to describe a way of relating to the Creator of the Cosmos, who is unknowable, except for what He reveals to us. Because of His great love for us, He has invited us to walk with Him on this

---

[2] Thomas Merton, *New Seeds of Contemplation* (New York: New Directions Books, 2007), pg. 6

long journey of discovery. It is only in walking that we begin to understand His activity in our lives. It has taken me many years of practicing contemplative prayer to begin to define or describe it. And its meaning continues to evolve as my relationship with Jesus deepens. Hold your questions and uncertainty before God, and the Holy Spirit will faithfully instruct and guide you.

In 1 Thessalonians 5:23, Paul prays for the church:

> Now may the God of peace Himself sanctify you completely; and may your whole **spirit**, **soul**, and **body** be preserved blameless at the coming of our Lord Jesus Christ.

I find it helpful to describe how each of these parts of our being, as described by Paul, is engaged in contemplative prayer:

Body – (our physical body). We make time in our day, find a physical location where we can sit alone in quiet, and learn to still our bodies. Here we wait with Jesus and with expectant hearts.

Soul – (our mind, affections, and will; what makes us a human individual; our heart) We will learn to quiet our minds. We then descend below our mind's thoughts, desires, and will, in order to meet with God at a deeper level than the human soul. In this interaction, our souls are transformed and conformed to the will of God.

Spirit – (God's life-giving breath within us) We believe by faith that the Holy Spirit is communicating with our spirits in ways that go beyond the limitations of our human mind. Here is where deep, transformational communion with God takes place, even though we can't see, smell, taste, or feel it. As Jesus told the

Samaritan woman at the well: *God is Spirit, and those who worship Him must worship in spirit and truth.* (John 4:24)

A broad definition combining these three parts of our being may be: contemplative prayer is a posture of waiting where we disengage our mind and thoughts as we sit quietly in humility before our Creator. He meets us in this place and communes with our spirit, which transforms our entire life.

Contemplative prayer is much more than just an exercise of the mind. It is based upon an attitude of the heart that compels us to approach God with humility and expectation. We believe He is Holy[3], 'other than,' beyond our human capacity to grasp or understand. Of course, some of us can indeed 'sense' God's presence with our physical senses, as there are no limitations to how He may choose to reveal Himself. But for many of us, most of the time, we must exercise faith to sit in God's presence, believing He is there and desires to be with us.

We assume this posture of our heart by faith, believing that He excitedly waits for us at the table described in Psalm 23:5, *You prepare a table before me in the presence of my enemies; You anoint my head with oil; My cup runs over.* We will discuss additional postures of our hearts that are important in Chapter 5.

Father Thomas Dubay in *Fire Within* defines contemplative prayer as,

---

[3] The Hebrew and Greek definitions of Holy include: of God; set apart; sacred; different from the world

> Christic (Christ-centered) contemplation is nothing less than a deep love communion with the triune God. By depth here we mean a knowing loving that we cannot produce but only receive. It is not merely a mentally expressed "I love you." It is a wordless awareness and love that we of ourselves cannot initiate or prolong.[4]

He summarizes thoughts from the sixteenth-century contemplative, Teresa of Avila,

> For [St. Teresa], contemplation is an experienced, mutual presence, "an intimate sharing between friends," a being alone with God who loves us. Hence, this prayer is a mutual presence of two in love, and in this case the Beloved dwells within... For Teresa this indwelling presence is the focal point of prayer: wherever God is, there is heaven, a fullness of glory. We are to find Him deep within ourselves... We need no wings, only a place of silence where we can be alone and center our gaze on Guests within.[5]

God initiates and draws us into this deep relationship by His grace. We cannot will ourselves into this type of love relationship. Instead, we make ourselves available and allow the Holy Spirit, in His timing, to draw us more deeply.

Again, summarizing St. Teresa's writing, Dubay adds,

---

[4] Thomas Dubay, S.M., *Fire Within* (San Francisco: Ignatius Press, 1989) pg. 57
[5] Ibid, pg. 58

> The fire of ecstatic prayer is so completely a divine, unmerited gift that she plays "no part in obtaining even a spark of it."[6]

Thomas Merton adds,

> True contemplation is not a psychological trick but a theological grace. It can come to us only as a gift, and not as a result of our own clever use of spiritual techniques.[7]

We cannot rush or provoke Him to meet our perceived needs in this place. We can only wait, be available, and respond.

Contemplation can be described as *seeing face to face, without the glass, reflecting darkly* (1 Corinthians 13:12). It's an obedient response to His drawing us to Himself. We are responding to God's call in our hearts to seek His face, just like David was instructed in Psalm 27:8. *When You said, "Seek My Face," My heart said to You, "Your face, Lord, I will seek."* Sitting before our God in obedience and humility, we begin to experience undistorted reality.

Contemplative prayer is also described and encouraged in scripture. David's psalms include several statements regarding waiting silently in the presence of God, for God. For example, Psalm 62:1 says: *Truly my soul silently waits for God; from Him comes my salvation.* In Psalm 27, David concludes in verse 14, *Wait on the Lord; be of good*

---

[6] Thomas Dubay, S.M., *Fire Within*, pg. 59
[7] Thomas Merton, *Contemplative Prayer* (New York: Random House, 2014) pg. 70

courage, and He shall strengthen your heart; Wait, I say, on the Lord!

From the Sons of Korah, Psalm 46:10 says, *Be still, and know that I am God.* And Habakkuk 2:20 instructs us, *But the Lord is in His holy temple. Let all the earth keep silence before Him.*

I am also drawn to Moses in Exodus, Chapter 24. In verses 15 & 16, the Lord called Moses up onto Mount Sinai. The fire and smoke cloud of His presence covered Mount Sinai for six days while Moses waited outside the cloud. On the seventh day, YHWH called Moses from the midst of the cloud into His presence, where He remained for forty days and nights and received the 10 commandments. What did Moses do for six days before the cloud of His presence? Scripture does not give us details, but it seems reasonable to me that for a significant part of those six days, he just waited quietly, alone in the presence of the Almighty, waiting for YHWH to speak. That is contemplative prayer.

Throughout the remainder of this primer, we will continue to build upon these descriptions of contemplative prayer. As you pursue your own contemplative prayer life, you will begin to develop your own meaningful description based on your experience. Your description of this form of prayer, however, will undoubtedly grow and change as your relationship with your Savior grows and deepens.

Meditation

Contemplative prayer and meditation are related. In fact, some early century contemplatives speak of them interchangeably as one leads to the other and vice versa.

Both are necessary, scriptural forms of prayer, and one is not better or more important than the other. Prayer is a dynamic, living encounter with God that includes many forms of communication. Our Lord's creative nature is beyond our ability to comprehend[8], and while praying, we often fluidly move from one activity to another.

These forms of prayer differ in the way we engage our hearts and minds and utilize scripture or other literature. As we have discussed, the practice of contemplative prayer helps to disengage our minds and thoughts. We practice sitting in God's presence in faith, eliminating thoughts, and trusting that our communication with Him is beyond our ability to comprehend. Meditation, on the other hand, purposefully engages our mind and thoughts. Through this process, we ingest what we are meditating on until these things become a part of us. Learning and memorization can be byproducts of this activity. This is a great gift from our Creator.

Scripture clearly instructs us to meditate upon God's Word. Psalm 1:2 instructs us:

> But his (the blessed person's) delight is in the law of the Lord, and in His law, he meditates day and night.

And YHWH instructed Joshua:

> This Book of the Law shall not depart from your mouth but you shall meditate in it day and night, that you may observe to do according to all that is written in it. **(Joshua 1:8)**

---

[8] Ephesians 3:8-10

Here, the Hebrew word translated *meditate* can also mean to moan, utter, and speak. He was instructed to continually repeat these words day and night, either out loud or under his breath.

Jesus continually referenced the Old Testament in His teachings. This means He spent much time studying and meditating on these scriptures. For example, in Luke 4:16-21, while in His childhood synagogue in Nazareth, He reads from the scroll of Isaiah about the Servant who would save Israel and the Gentiles. In verse 21, He says, *"Today this Scripture is fulfilled in your hearing,"* announcing Himself as the Servant and Redeemer of Israel. I am not claiming to understand how Jesus knew He was the Servant in Isaiah's prophecies; however, it is clear from Luke's gospel that Jesus meditated on and studied the Hebrew Bible as a child.

> Now so it was that after three days they found Him in the temple, sitting in the midst of the teachers, both listening to them and asking them questions. And all who heard Him were astonished at His understanding and answers… And Jesus increased in wisdom and stature, and in favor with God and men. **(Luke 2:46 & 52)**

Clearly, meditation was an important part of Jesus' prayer life with His Father, as it is with ours. We cannot rush this activity. The quantity of the Scripture we read is irrelevant. Allowing the Holy Spirit time to speak to us through these sacred words is the goal.

Different types of meditative prayer are necessary and beneficial. We will describe two types below that are important to nurture a deepening prayer life.

Borrowing language from seventeenth-century French contemplative, Jeanne Guyon, the first is "praying the Scripture" and the second "beholding the Lord." She describes these activities as having different purposes.

> In "praying the Scripture" you are seeking to find the Lord in what you are reading, in the very words themselves. In this path, therefore, the content of the Scripture is the focal point of your attention. Your purpose is to take everything from the passage that unveils the Lord to you.
>
> In "beholding the Lord," you come to the Lord in a totally different way. Perhaps at this point, I need to share with you the greatest difficulty you will have in waiting upon the Lord. It has to do with our mind. The mind has a very strong tendency to stray away from the Lord. Therefore, as you come before your Lord to sit in His presence, beholding Him, make use of the Scripture to quiet your mind.[9]

Praying the scripture

Praying the scripture is often referred to as *Lectio Divina*. This is Latin for Divine Reading. This is a way of purposefully reading the Bible to encounter the Holy Spirit through its living words. Sister Joan Chittister's description is helpful,

> Monastic *lectio* is the practice of reading small passages daily – a page, a paragraph, a sentence

---

[9] Jeanne Guyon, *Experiencing the Depths of Jesus Christ* (Jacksonville: SeedSowers Publishing, 1975) pg. 9

– and then milking meaning for meaning any word or phrase or situation that interests or provokes me there. Then the soul wrestling begins. The question becomes: why does this word or passage mean something to me? Why is this word or situation bothering me? What does it mean to me, say to me? What feeling does it bring out in me? *Lectio* is a slow, reflective process that takes us down below the preoccupations of the moment, the distractions of the day to that place where the soul holds the residue of life.[10]

This activity includes both reading and praying the Scripture.

Beholding the Lord

The second type, beholding the Lord, is an avenue to contemplation. We've discussed that God dwells in the center of our being, beyond our mind and understanding. He resides in our spirit and is constantly drawing us to Himself in this place deep within. Jeanne Guyon relates His constant drawing to a magnetic attraction. "He draws you more and more powerfully to Himself."[11]

Beholding the Lord through meditation is a turning inward towards the center. As we are drawn deeper into meditation, we can enter more easily into contemplation.

---

[10] Joan Chittister, *Illuminated Life*, pg. 76
[11] Jeanne Guyon, *Union with God* (Jacksonville; SeedSowers Publishing, 1999) pg. 3

His Constant Call

In fact, my experience is that contemplation often follows this type of meditation.

As we engage in slow, quiet, deep meditation where we are moved or touched by a scripture or phrase, we are naturally led to contemplation. While meditating, we are thinking about God, an attribute, a scripture that describes Him, or a phrase that demonstrates His love. As we sit thinking about Him, He will draw us to a place where we stop thinking and just sit with Him, in Him. In faith, we behold Him. This is contemplation. We usually then move back to meditation and begin once again thinking about Him. This back-and-forth can last as long as He draws us. We'll discuss this again as we describe interior silence in Chapter 4.

In Psalm 27:4 (AMP), David speaks of both contemplation and meditation,

> One thing have I asked of the Lord, that will I seek, inquire for, and require: that I may dwell in the house of the Lord [in His presence] all the days of my life, to behold and gaze upon the beauty of the Lord and to meditate, consider, and inquire in his temple.

The cry of David's heart is to actively meditate on and consider the Lord as well as behold Him and gaze upon His beauty (contemplation).

It is in beholding Jesus that we are transformed:

> And we all, with unveiled face, beholding the glory of the Lord, are being transformed into the same image from one degree of glory to another. **(2 Corinthians 3:18 AMP)**

The contemplative life

Contemplative prayer leads to a contemplative life. The goal of contemplative prayer is a deeper, more real relationship with Jesus. The inevitable outcome of this relationship is that what begins alone in our prayer closet continues throughout our entire, sometimes mundane lives. The contemplative life gives us a greater awareness of His presence all day long, not only during our prayer time. This is the desire He has placed in our hearts: to allow the Holy Spirit to daily increase our capacity to know Him and live in the fullness of the life He has given us.

As Joan Chittister puts it,

> Contemplation is not a private devotion; it is a way of life. It changes the way we think. It shapes the way we live. It challenges the way we talk, and where we go, and what we do. We do not "contemplate" or "not contemplate." We live the contemplative life.[12]

Not only are our hearts transformed as we sit before Him, but He is simultaneously expanding our capacity to recognize and experience Him. As we allow Him time to reveal closed rooms in our hearts and we give Him access to those dark places, He sweeps them clean. He then fills those spaces with His truth. This expands our capacity to recognize and love Him more. This is the win-win of His grace.

Over time, contemplative prayer impacts our entire being and changes every area of our lives. The way we

---

[12] Joan Chittister, *Illuminated Life*, pg. 75

perceive life and how we live is renewed. It instills hope and transforms our entire personality, including our social and private lives. It must be this way if we are truly in the presence of the Lord.

How does contemplative prayer change us?

Contemplative prayer reveals reality. The Holy Spirit removes the scales from our eyes and expands our capacity to recognize His glory all around us.

Father Ronald Rolheiser describes the impacts of contemplative prayer:

> The quality of awareness, or lack of it, in ordinary life is what contemplation is all about. Contemplation is about waking up. Simply defined, to be contemplative is to experience an event fully, in all its aspects … we are in contemplation when we stand before reality and experience it without the limits and distortions that are created by narcissism, pragmatism, and excessive restlessness. To be contemplative is to be fully awake to all dimensions within ordinary experience. When we are fully awake to ordinary experience, it brings with it a certain *contuition* (unconscious awareness) of God.[13]

The Holy Spirit changes many aspects of our perception as He renews our minds. He purifies our awareness, especially of others, while at the same time enhancing our individuality. He makes us less pragmatic, teaching

---

[13] Ronald Rolheiser, *The Shattered Lantern* (New York: Crossroad Publishing Co., 2001), pg.23

us to wonder. Our natural instinct for astonishment is restored. He enables us to see reality more clearly, so that we find contentment and rest.

I am convinced that almost 25 years of practicing contemplative prayer has changed my life in real, tangible ways. To be clear, it's been a challenging path, and I have not achieved any degree of perfection. I agree with Thomas Merton, "We do not want to be beginners. But let us be convinced of the fact that we will never be anything else but beginners, all our life!"[14] Still, my life has changed.

My hectic life, driven by vacillating emotions, somehow slows down to recognize that I have choices throughout the day. Not all the time, but more and more, I am reminded that I have a decision to choose life or death:

- a choice to believe He is near this very moment;
- a choice to receive this experience as an opportunity to allow Him to reveal my heart and change me;
- a choice to prefer others more than myself;
- a choice to remember Him and rest.

Or I can choose death through worry, fear, and anxiety.

Learning to quiet my mind continues to be the most challenging exercise in my life. After countless early morning hours that seem like wasted time, there has been improvement, and my soul is now far more

---

[14] Thomas Merton, *Contemplative Prayer*, pg. 13

obedient to the command, "BE STILL!" While stress and fear have not been entirely eliminated from my days, these unwanted pests distract me far less frequently than they used to.

Our developing history with Jesus is key to continuing on this path. Over time, we learn to trust His faithfulness and begin to believe His heart is for us. He will be found by those who seek Him (Jeremiah 29:13). By His grace, it has become easier to remember Him and, therefore, acknowledge His presence throughout the day. Bottom line is that I talk with Him more, often out loud, as I believe He is near. His presence has become more real in my life.

Chapter 3

THE ANCIENT PATHS OF CONTEMPLATIVE PRAYER

Everyone is capable of praying, but many have the mistaken idea that they are not called to prayer. Just as we are called to salvation, we are called to prayer…There is only one requirement, though, that you must follow at all times. It will not interfere with outward actions. It may be practiced by princes, kings, priests, soldiers, children, and laborers. This simple requirement is that you must learn to pray from your heart and not your head.[1]

In this chapter, we will look at the mystical tradition of contemplative prayer. This tradition has provided instruction and encouragement for our church for more than two decades. It is sometimes referred to as the Catholic tradition, as centuries of writings from Catholic contemplatives have provided instruction and guidance for generations of believers. Written instruction and experience from these saints have helped blaze a trail for modern-day practitioners of contemplative prayer.

---

[1] Jeanne Guyon, *Experiencing God Through Prayer* (New Kensington: Whitaker House, 1984) pgs. 19-21

Additionally, many Protestant and modern-day Catholic authors have also impacted our community. All these sojourners have provided a rich library to assist and encourage believers in contemplative prayer. Clearly, these are ancient paths as described in Jeremiah 6:16 (AMP):

> Thus says the Lord: "Stand by the roads and look; ask for the ancient paths, Where the good way is; then walk in it, and you will find rest for your souls."

A brief discussion of the mystical tradition will be helpful as we continue to build upon our description of contemplative prayer. While much of this written guidance can be difficult for modern readers, there is truth to be mined through meditation and perseverance. If you are anything like me and desire to better understand these teachings and how they apply to your life, you'll need to come back to them time and again over many years. As we grow in the practice of contemplative prayer, the teachings of these saints will make more sense. My goal is to summarize some key ideas of this tradition from resources that have directly impacted our church community and my own journey.

Mysticism

Mysticism describes direct union or communion with God through deep meditation or contemplation. Christian mysticism is centered on Jesus. While this term may intimidate or scare some of us, it is simply one way to describe our interactions with this God we cannot see with our eyes or hear with our ears. It's a way of describing our communication and interaction with the Holy Spirit that is beyond our physical senses.

Mystical experiences are spiritual encounters with our supernatural Creator, who is holy, which means "other than."

I like Ronald Rolheiser's description of mysticism from *The Shattered Lantern* because it removes any sense of elitism or exclusivity and makes clear that all Christians in a loving relationship with God can be mystics:

> ...mysticism is, in fact, a very ordinary experience, an experience open to all and had by all. Simply defined, mysticism is being touched by God (or anything else) in a way that is inchoate,[2] namely, in a way that goes beyond what we can think, express, pictorially imagine, and even clearly feel.[3]

Mystical experiences are not reserved for some elite group of uber-spiritual individuals, but rather, all believers who have felt or experienced a touch from the loving Father. Some contemplatives describe a "dark knowledge" that often accompanies these deep spiritual interactions with God. Dark knowledge simply means the encounter is beyond or above our understanding. It is indescribable or indefinable, and therefore, dark. We only know that the touch of God was real and that we have been impacted deeply.

The definition by John Crowder in *Mystical Union* is also helpful:

---

[2] Inchoate: imperfectly formed or formulated (Merriam-Webster Dictionary)
[3] Ronald Rolheiser, *The Shattered Lantern* (New York: The Crossroad Publishing Company, 2001) pg. 80

> I define mysticism as: an experience of union with God – a consciousness of the reality of God. The belief that the reality of God can be infused through subjective experience.[4]

Faith is required to acknowledge and receive a mystical encounter.

The mystical tradition

The mystical tradition is centered around the pursuit of purity of heart as described in Matthew 5:8. Jesus said, *Blessed are the pure of heart, for they shall see God*. It began with the Desert Fathers. These were third-century Christians desiring to follow Jesus and His teachings. They sold their possessions, gave their money to the poor, and turned to solitary lives in the desert on their quest to purify their hearts. Most would emerge from the desert after some time and begin their ministry. Others remained in the desert. This was the birth of monasticism,[5] and these were the first Christian monks.

The lifestyle and writings of the Desert Fathers significantly impacted the early, growing Christian church. Their teachings resulted in a long, deep tradition of contemplative prayer and mysticism in the Catholic church that includes much written guidance. Monks and nuns living in small communities were especially given to monastic lives of servanthood and prayer. These individuals are often referred to as mystics. They lived radical lives of isolation, detachment, and obedience that

---

[4] John Crowder, *Mystical Union* (Marylhurst: Sons of Thunder Ministries and Publications, 2016) pg. 12

[5] Monasticism - a religious way of life in which one renounces worldly pursuits to devote oneself fully to spiritual work.

modern believers may find challenging to emulate. The truths they have discovered while walking with Jesus, however, are timeless and very helpful.

A life of purity and humility is a key cornerstone necessary for contemplation in this tradition. Father Thomas Dubay summarizes the writings and teachings of two 16th-century Catholic mystics, Teresa of Avila and John of the Cross, in *Fire Within*.

> Without humility, detachment, and sound doctrine, there is no deep communion with the Lord. There could not be, for quality of prayer correlates with quality of life, that is, evangelical life, not a naturalistic substitute…. Life-style and prayer grow or diminish together. If people today or in any age lack mystical prayer, it is not because it has been tried and found lacking. It is the Gospel that has not been tried.[6]

Detachment

Detachment is a key to the pursuit of purity of heart in the mystical tradition. The mystics taught that detachment from all worldly possessions was necessary to obtain inner freedom to love God completely. They go beyond possessions, however, to include things like self-centered desires, knowledge, human appetites, and anything that brings gratification. These things aren't necessarily bad in and of themselves. Our soul's desire to possess and find pleasure in them apart from God is the real issue. The mystics believed that no one can attain complete joy in God without giving up self-

---

[6] Thomas Dubay, S.M., *Fire Within* (San Francisco: Ignatius Press, 1989) pg. 9

centered pleasures in things lesser than God. Father Dubay summarizes the teachings of John of the Cross,

> John is simply observing that if anyone is serious about loving God totally, he must willingly entertain no self-centered pursuit of finite things sought for themselves, that is, devoid of honest direction to God, our sole end and purpose. St. Paul makes exactly the same point when he tells the Corinthians that whatever they eat or drink, or whatever else they do, they are to do all for the glory of God. Whatever does mean whatever, and all does mean all. [7]

John of the Cross describes our love for God as being above all things in our lives,

> Herein is fulfilled the precept of love, namely, that we are to love him above all things. And if this love is to be perfect, we must live in perfect detachment and in a special emptiness of all things.[8]

Brother Lawrence, a 17th-century Catholic mystic, wrote one of the most famous Christian guides on prayer, *Practicing the Presence of God*. His challenging words are profoundly simple.

> So, I resolved to give all for ALL (*God*). Then I gave myself wholly to God; I renounced everything that was not His. I did this to deal with my sins and because of my love for Him.

---

[7] Thomas Dubay, S.M., *Fire Within*, pg. 134
[8] John of the Cross, *The Living Flame of Love* (London: Society for Promoting Christian Knowledge, 2017) pgs. 67-68

> I began to live as if there were nothing, absolutely nothing but Him. So upon this earth I began to seek to live as though there were only the Lord and me in the whole world.[9]

This is the heart of the teachings of the early mystics regarding earthly possessions. Worldly possessions, and more importantly, our attachment to them, are a primary hindrance to contemplative prayer and a life of deep intimacy with God. Thomas Merton summarizes these ideas:

> The secret of interior peace is detachment. Recollection (*a gentle awareness of God*) is impossible for the man who is dominated by all the confused and changing desires of his own will. And even if those desires reach out for the good things of the interior life, for recollection, for peace, for the pleasures of prayer, if they are no more than the natural and selfish desires, they will make recollection difficult and even impossible.[10]

These saints are repeating what Jesus taught regarding worldly possessions in the gospels. For example, in Luke 14:33 (AMP), Jesus says,

> So then, none of you can be My disciple who does not [carefully consider the cost and then for My sake] give up all his own possessions.

---

[9] Brother Lawrence and Frank Laubach, *Practicing His Presence* (Jacksonville: SeedSowers Publishing, 1973) pg. 59, *italics mine*

[10] Thomas Merton, *New Seeds of Contemplation* (New York: New Directions Books, 2007) pgs. 207-208, *italics mine*

The premise is that "only the free can love, and only the completely free can love unreservedly."[11] This was certainly the example Jesus lived while on earth. He had no place to call home[12], no apparent employment while He ministered, and we are told of no earthly possessions He carried with Him. It is hard to imagine this kind of life in our modern world. The mystics, however, believed that detachment was a necessary purification process enabling humans to become divinely transformed. Does this mean we have to be totally detached in order for God to transform us? Absolutely, not. In fact, it is God's grace that enables us to detach from things in our lives as He is transforming us.

We can willingly purge our lives of some things that hinder attention to God. It's not too hard to think of items in our own lives that usurp our time, energy, and money that could be reduced or eliminated. Possessions and activities that have become common in our comfortable lives, like entertainment, social media, technology, shopping, etc., can hinder prioritizing our relationship with God. The Holy Spirit is faithful to highlight anything in our lives that is occupying a place that God desires. Letting them go, however, can be challenging and requires a reprioritization of our lives.

Other distractions in our lives, especially non-material, innate items, are more difficult or even impossible for us to eliminate and require God's purification and grace. Sitting before the Lord in silence and solitude enables the believer to lose sight of temporal things of

---

[11] Thomas Dubay, *Fire Within*, pg. 131
[12] Luke 9:58, Matthew 8:20

the world as focus shifts to the eternal rewards of heaven. Over time, we are enabled to detach from things that have an improper place in our lives as we simultaneously grow in love for the Lord.

The mystics describe a detachment that is difficult for me to wrap my head around in my affluent life. Their message is clear: anything in our lives that is not of God hinders us from God. It has been my experience that the detachment described by the mystics is a painful process. While the Holy Spirit is most kind and gentle, being stripped of all things that hold us back from a deeper relationship with God often hurts and has been, at times, confusing. These include innate desires we are born with, as well as things learned throughout our lives. Even good things in our lives, like His amazing creation, can become a hindrance that holds us back from God if we seek peace in them instead of the Creator. Good things can truly be the enemy of the best things. Wisdom and grace are required to determine which is which.

John of the Cross' mystical instruction

The teachings of John of the Cross are representative of the teachings of the mystical tradition. Many of his writings have been lost, but those that remain provide a detailed path for the work of contemplative prayer. I do not claim to be an expert on John's writings and confess that they are very challenging for me to read and digest. What I have gleaned, however, is profound and very helpful. His description of the transformative work of the Holy Spirit in our lives as we grow in a deeper relationship with God has been especially helpful. John's poetic writings communicate important truths about human struggles and how the Holy Spirit transforms our souls to bring us to more complete faith in God.

John describes the work of the Holy Spirit as "dark nights" of the soul and the spirit.

> ...it must be known that, for a soul to attain to the state of perfection, it has ordinarily first to pass through two principal kinds of night, which spiritual persons call purgations [13] or purifications of the soul; and here we call them nights, for in both of them the soul journeys, as it were, by night, in darkness.[14]

The Lord leads us through these in order to eliminate inappropriate desires by purging or removing them from our hearts. Similar to dark knowledge described above, dark nights are works of the Holy Spirit that are difficult to describe (dark) and include an emptying or being purged that is painful (night). The outcome, however, results in greater faith and trust in the goodness of God along with an increased awareness of His presence in our lives.

John is clear that these dark nights are not well-defined seasons of our lives with a beginning and end, but there are signposts that we can use to identify this work of the Holy Spirit. Additionally, we do not simply move from one dark night to the other as we grow and mature. Rather, these are fluid seasons, and we may

---

[13] Purgation: the act of purging. Purging: to make free of something unwanted; to get rid of. (Merriam-Webster Dictionary)

[14] Saint John of the Cross, *Ascent of Mount Carmel* (Eastford: Martino Fine Books, 2016) pg. 17-18

move in and out of them as the Holy Spirit leads. The point of including John's example is not the process he describes as much as what needs to be transformed in our lives and how the Holy Spirit sometimes works.

It is also worth restating here that we believe union with God has already been attained by Jesus through the work of the cross in our lives.[15] Our old man has been crucified and we are growing in the knowledge and experience of what we already have.[16] These dark nights are a way the Holy Spirit clears the clutter of our human hearts in order to experience the reality of what we already have as believers.

My personal journey has been similar to John's poetic description of the transformational work of contemplative prayer through the dark nights. The summary below highlights important and helpful points that were beneficial for me and our church community. He may work in you differently.

Eternity in our hearts

We enter this world with a deep desire for intimacy with God. Father Rolheiser summarizes this desire in every human being:

> For John [of the Cross], just as for Plato and Augustine before him, we are fired into life with a madness that comes from the gods and which leaves us incurably restless, seeking,

---

[15] 1 Corinthians 3:16; Colossians 2:9-10; 1 John 4:15
[16] Romans 6:6; Galatians 2:20; Galatians 5:24; Ephesians 2:1&4-10

longing, and insatiably drawn to a beauty, goodness, truth and unity beyond ourselves.[17]

Solomon also describes this,

> He has also planted eternity [a sense of divine purpose] in the human heart [a mysterious longing which nothing under the sun can satisfy, except God] – yet man cannot find out (comprehend, grasp) what God has done (His overall plan) from the beginning to the end **(Ecclesiastes 3:11 AMP).**

This internal desire creates a tension within us as we crave eternity and the infinite within our finite humanity. This longing is God's life within us as He is drawing human beings unto Himself. A deep relationship with God is the only relief for this incurable restlessness. John describes two veils that separate us from this full communion with God: the veil of the senses and the veil of the spirit. Through the work of the Holy Spirit, as we sit with Him in silence and solitude, these veils must be stripped. This, according to John, is what occurs through the dark nights. He instructs that this process is what the spiritual journey is all about.

The dark night of the senses

This dark night purifies the five human senses of all their "disordered seekings."[18] John tells us that we are born with the dominant instinct for preserving and bringing pleasure to the self. That is, the primary motivation for our actions is focused on self-

---

[17] Ronald Rolheiser, *The Shattered Lantern*, pg. 83
[18] Thomas Dubay, *Fire Within*, pg. 159

preservation and comfort. For example, what are your favorite "comfort foods?" These are foods we eat because they bring us pleasure and comfort. These foods aren't bad in themselves, but John would argue they are harmful when our desires are inordinate or control us and we enjoy them outside of the Giver. The Holy Spirit works in us in order to remove our dependency upon our sensual[19] pleasures. The first dark night is meant to purify our selfish desire for pleasure and gratification, and instead, live for God alone.

Our soul is purified through this dark night as the Holy Spirit begins to eliminate the pleasure these things used to bring. For example, we may find a form of entertainment that used to bring us rest and enjoyment, no longer provides those comforts. When these pleasures are eliminated, in desperation, we turn to the promises of Jesus. These include peace, rest, and life. Deep down, we know that only intimacy with God can provide the satisfaction we seek in these other activities and possessions. In the dark night, we experience the pain of stripping away the selfish motivation of our senses, and we are left feeling naked and bare. It is in this place that we finally turn to God as our primary source of comfort and life. Like the disciples in John 6:68, we cry, *where else can we go? You alone have the words of life.*

Simultaneously, John says, as things that bring us pleasure are purified, we are also being matured through the experience of spiritual dryness. God dries

---

[19] Sensual: relating to or consisting in the gratification of the senses or the indulgence of appetite. (Merriam-Webster Dictionary)

up the experience of satisfaction in prayer in order to help us mature and teach us to walk in greater faith. John says that God sees we have grown a little,

> ...so He sets them down from His arms and teaches them to walk on their own feet, which they feel to be very strange, for everything seems to be going wrong with them.[20]

A new motivation for our actions is needed to move beyond the attainment of pleasure and self-satisfaction.

Love of and for Jesus becomes that motivation through His example in the gospels. We will begin to act in obedience to Jesus's motivation and no longer by our need for pleasure. We become freed from the neediness that causes us to project ourselves and our needs before everything and everybody else.

John summarizes the primary effect of passing through this dark night as the knowledge of our inadequacies and total need for God. Like Jesus spoke to the church of the Laodiceans, we learn we are *...wretched, miserable, poor, blind, and naked.* **(Revelation 3:17)**

> ...this virtue of self-knowledge, which is so excellent and so necessary, considering itself now as nothing and experiencing no satisfaction in itself; for it sees that it does nothing of itself neither can do anything. [21]

Not only does this self-knowledge purify the senses, but it simultaneously leads to greater humility, and we

---

[20] St. John of the Cross, *Dark Night of the Soul*, (Mineola: Dover Publications, 2003) pg. 21
[21] Ibid, pg. 31

begin to approach God with more respect and reverence. Pride is purged from the soul when it recognizes that only God can provide all that it needs. We are awakened to a new awareness of the greatness and excellence of God. This new self-awareness leads to a greater love of our neighbors. We begin to esteem them and judge them less as we are more aware of our own wretchedness. John says,

> It (*the soul*) is aware only of its own wretchedness, which it keeps before its eyes to such an extent that it never forgets it, nor takes occasion to set its eyes on anyone else. [22]

After passing through this dark night, our soul is renewed, and we move beyond self-centered motivation to a desire to serve God out of love for Him. John uses the metaphor of our soul as a household where the sensual nature exists. After the dark night, John says, "the house remains at rest and quiet."[23]

The dark night of the spirit

John describes the second phase of the purification as far more demanding than the first. The first night purged only the senses. The purpose of the dark night of the spirit is to purify our intellect and will, which we rely on for knowledge, love, and security. John refers to these as the roots in our soul that must be addressed in order to grow in spiritual awareness of God's goodness and faithfulness.

---

[22] St. John of the Cross, *Dark Night of the Soul*, pg. 34
[23] Ibid, pg. 38

> ...He is purging the soul, annihilating it, emptying it, or consuming in it (even as fire consumes the mouldiness and the rust of metal) all the affections and imperfect habits which it has concentrated in its whole life. Since these are deeply rooted in the substance of the soul, it is wont to suffer great undoing and inward torment, besides the said poverty and emptiness, natural and spiritual...[24]

Father Rolheiser adds,

> What the dark night of the spirit does is to purify our heads, hearts, and person in such a way that these now relate to everything, not through their normal propensity for conceptual understanding, possession, and security, but through faith, charity, and hope.[25]

This season can be painfully disorienting as our memory, imagination, intellect, and will are all being purged and transformed. For example, we may discover that patterns of thoughts and actions in response to certain situations no longer provide the sense of security they used to. We are being moved from human thought and reasoning to divine obedience. What we have grown accustomed to, especially regarding prayer, no longer brings the peace and joy we have previously known. Ways we have previously experienced His presence and love are suddenly ineffective and barren. In fact, we believe God has become displeased with us and has even

---

[24] St. John of the Cross, *Dark Night of the Soul*, pgs. 51-52
[25] Ronald Rolheiser, *The Shattered Lantern*, pg. 92

abandoned us. John uses strong language to describe this season of purification, including an "oppressive undoing."

All the while, however, John tells us the soul in this process,

> ...feels itself to be keenly and sharply wounded in strong Divine love, and to have a certain realization and foretaste of God...The spirit feels itself here to be deeply and passionately in love, for this spiritual enkindling produces the passion of love...This love has in it something of union with God.[26]

John says that through this dark night, "God raises up profound blessings in the soul out of darkness."[27] The primary fruit is an abounding and growing love for God. A love that is consuming. A love that motivates the believer to serve with increased generosity. This love also becomes the main source of hope and strength in the believer's life.

Our vision is purified as we no longer see through our intellect or memory.

> ...our heads, hearts, and egos, deprived of their normal way of relating to what is beyond them, then begin to rely on faith, hope, and charity as the prisms through which they relate.[28]

We begin to recognize that something within has changed. Our way of perceiving people and things

---

[26] St. John of the Cross, *Dark Night of the Soul*, pg. 68
[27] Ibid, pg. 54
[28] Ronald Rolheiser, *The Shattered Lantern*, pg. 95

around us becomes more pure and less possessive. We begin to see and appreciate people and things for their own beauty, not for what they provide to us. Our "gaze of possessiveness, lust, and jealousy turns into the gaze of admiration"[29] and appreciation.

Father Rolheiser summarizes this work of purification as necessary to restore us to the fullness of wonder,

> Unless our normal way of understanding is transformed so that we begin to understand more by not understanding than by understanding, we will never truly stand before each other and the world in wonder.[30]

Passing through these dark nights expands our capacity to see His glory everywhere!

Summary

G.K. Chesterton wrote that "the greatest of all illusions is the illusion of familiarity."[31] Religion fills our minds with knowledge about God until He becomes familiar. This is a dangerous, arrogant, and completely incorrect conclusion to arrive at. While there is guidance from those who have gone before, the contemplative path is a journey with our Savior into the darkness of the unknown. We learn to embrace our inability to know God's ways and instead trust His goodness. Letting go of our need for control allows us freedom to return, as children, to the wonder and awe of our Creator's arms. Father Rolheiser is correct when he says,

---

[29] Ronald Rolheiser, *The Shattered Lantern*, pg. 95
[30] Ibid, pg. 102
[31] Ibid, pg. 127

> Familiarity is also the death of respect, wonder, and awe. When our minds, hearts, and imaginations are no longer poised for surprise and astonishment, then we no longer have a healthy fear of God or indeed of each other. A healthy fear of God means living in such a way that nothing becomes too familiar to us.[32]

Regardless of what motivates us in prayer, Father Thomas Dubay sums up the ache that compels us to approach our Lord contemplatively in *The Evidential Power of Beauty*:

> You and I, each and every one of us without exception, can be defined as an aching need for the infinite. Some people realize this; some do not.... If these people (*those who do not realize this*) allow themselves a moment of reflective silence (which they seldom do), they notice a still, small voice whispering, "*Is this all there is?*" They begin to sense a thirst to love with abandon, without limit, without end, without lingering aftertastes of bitterness. In other words, their inner spirit is clamoring, even if confusedly, for unending beauty. How they and we respond to this inner outreach rooted in our deep spiritual soul is the most basic set of decisions we can make: they have eternal consequences.[33]

---

[32] Ronald Rolheiser, *The Shattered Lantern*, pgs. 127-128
[33] Thomas Dubay, S.M. *The Evidential Power of Beauty* (San Francisco: Ignatius Press, 1999) pg. 17

Chapter 4

The Secret Place, Solitude, and Interior Silence

The key to contemplation is making time and persevering...If one stays with this regularly, it can become a conduit for great peace and joy. Don't look for results, and don't give up. Those who don't want to know their real self and can't go past their own ego to the true center will not be successful.[1]

In this chapter, we will describe the secret place, solitude, and interior silence, which are primary disciplines of contemplative prayer. These three are closely related and difficult to separate because each is dependent upon the other. Most of us find these very challenging, especially in our busy, full lives. As we purpose in our hearts to make time and a place to meet with Jesus, it will get easier. Recognizing that this is a relationship that takes time is key. He is not in a hurry,

---

[1] Jacqueline Galloway, Reprinted from Volume 5, Number 4 of the Autumn 1990 issue of CARMELITE DIGEST (San Jose, 1990) https://ecatholic2000.com/pray/prayer2.shtml

and we will also learn to appreciate and even enjoy His pace.

The beginning

> For You formed my inward parts; You covered me in my mother's womb. I will praise You, for I am fearfully and wonderfully made; marvelous are Your works, and that my soul knows very well. My frame was not hidden from You, when I was made in secret, and skillfully wrought in the lowest parts of the earth. Your eyes saw my substance, being yet unformed. And in Your book they all were written, The days fashioned for me, When as yet there were none of them. **(Psalm 139:13-16)**

These are profound prophetic words written by King David thousands of years ago. We were known even before we were formed. What a staggering thought! And I believe we were created in the secret place of the womb, alone and likely in silence with our Creator. This is our beginning, before our beginning.

Imagine the peace and safety of the womb as we were being knit together. Alone, wrapped tightly in warmth and comfort, with only the beating of our mother's heart echoing constantly through our entire being. Perhaps this is the ultimate mystical experience that sets the stage for longing for communion with our Creator from the very beginning of our existence.

The internal pull to intimacy with God, then, can be seen as a longing to return to our 'beginning' with our Creator, to the place where we were conceived as Holy thought and then knit together, when all our days were written down in His book. This, I believe, is the great gift given to all human beings, a deep longing that fuels our desire for intimacy with God.

The secret place

> But you, when you pray, go into your room, and when you have shut your door, pray to your Father who is in the secret place; and your Father who sees in secret will reward you openly. **(Matthew 6:6)**

Before He told us how to pray, Jesus instructed us where to pray. He made it clear that the Father is waiting for us. This is the life-changing revelation of making time for God in the secret place: He is already there and waiting to meet with us! Jesus said so. What a fantastic truth! The moment I get to the secret place, I am in the immediate presence of my Father.

But where is the secret place, and how do we get there? These are intimidating questions, and the answers seem a bit confusing at first. The secret place is simply where He is. It is not a physical location, although identifying a location to seek Him is important. It's an interior meeting place that will become more real to us as we grow in prayer. A place of *inwardness* within our minds and hearts.

Author Calvin Miller captures the frustration of trying to explain this spiritual meeting place,

> Writing [about] inwardness is a task that has all the same frustrations I felt as a child, not being able to explain the magnificent Christ inside me. How can I tell you? How shall I define it? Inwardness defies all laws of space and time,

> and endows us with a life and destiny greater than our own. What we contain is more than what we are. It is heaven, immeasurable, love without dimensions: all in the confines of a fleshly frame. It is the fullness of purpose, without which there is no great purpose.[2]

What we contain is more than what we are! What a fantastic truth. For those of us who have confessed our trust in the lordship of Jesus, the fullness of the Holy Trinity dwells within us.[3] Jesus told His disciples at the last supper.

> If anyone loves Me, he will keep My word; and My Father will love Him, and We will come to him and make Our home with him. **(John 14:23)**

And

> "If you love Me, keep My commandments. And I will pray the Father, and He will give you another Helper, that He may abide with you forever—the Spirit of truth, whom the world cannot receive, because it neither sees Him nor knows Him; but you know Him, for He dwells with you and will be in you. **(John 14:15-17)**

This, I believe, is the secret place where the Father, Son, and Holy Spirit dwell within us. This is where I go to meet with my Savior. I try to descend out of my head and into my spirit.

---

[2] Calvin Miller, *The Table of Inwardness* (Downers Grove: Inter-Varsity Press, 1984) pgs. 12-13

[3] John 14:16-17; 1 Corinthians 6:19; Colossians 2:9

We are all created differently and with unique ways of communicating with God. Going to the secret place will look different for all of us. I happen to be very visual and have found that sometimes using my imagination is helpful. We will discuss this more in Chapter 7, but for now, as I describe my personal experience, many will find this technique foreign and unhelpful; that's okay. The main message is to ask the Holy Spirit to teach you how to get to your secret place. He is a great teacher!

Many years ago, I believe the Lord helped me to learn to descend from my head to my spirit (the secret place) through an impression in my imagination. It has been very helpful for me, especially at the beginning of this journey. It begins with an image of my feet descending a metal spiral staircase in some type of building. All I hear is the sound of my black shoes on the metal steps.

At the bottom of the stairs, I step off onto a sandy path that leaves the structure. I am now barefoot. The path takes me through some tall grasses on the edge of a beach. Dawn is just breaking through, so the morning light is gloomy. In the distance, I see a bright light that makes my heart beat faster as anticipation grows. I know Jesus is the light. He is my destination. My pace quickens, and when I get to Him, I fall to the ground and lay my head on His nail-scarred feet. I never see His face, but I am sure it's Him. I am now in the secret place with my Savior. It is here I find absolute safety and peace for my weary soul. I stay as long as I can; as long as He allows. Sometimes seconds, sometimes minutes or even an hour.

However, the Holy Spirit teaches us to find the secret place, be sure that over time we'll learn to access this place wherever and whenever we desire to respond to His call. There we wait for Him. This will be difficult at first, but we must trust He is drawing us and be patient. Perseverance is very important, as most days we will feel as though we are wasting our time, making no progress. A breakthrough will come, but not on our timetable. God is in control of this adventure and will reveal His secret place in His perfect timing. So, until then, we wait in faith, knowing that He is already waiting for us!

The secret place is not about a physical location, but finding a physical place to seek Him, especially when beginning this practice, is critical. As we grow in this discipline and learn to discern His voice, we will be drawn to other physical locations. At the beginning, however, we identify a physical place that is quiet and comfortable and begin to establish the discipline of meeting Him within.

Bob Sorge says,

> One of the best kept secrets of our faith is the blessedness and joy of cultivating a secret life with God… As you devote yourself to the secret place with God, He will birth something within you that will spread, in His time, to the four corners of your sphere… The secret place is the secret![4]

As we learn to go to the secret place, He will begin to reveal Himself and speak to our hearts.

---

[4] Bob Sorge, *Secrets of the Secret Place* (Kansas City: Oasis House, 2018), pgs. 4&6

Solitude

Why is solitude so important? Why do we need to get alone with God? Henri Nouwen says it well in *The Way of the Heart*,

> Solitude is the furnace of transformation. Without solitude we remain victims of our society and continue to be entangled in the illusions of the false self. Jesus Himself entered into this furnace.[5]

He goes on to describe the vulnerability of being alone with God,

> In solitude I get rid of my scaffolding: no friends to talk with, no telephone calls to make, no meetings to attend, no music to entertain, no books to distract, just me–naked, vulnerable, weak, sinful, deprived, broken–nothing.[6]

The solitude we seek is to be alone with our Savior. It is a posture of our heart that requires faith. Richard Foster addresses this in *Celebration of Discipline*,

> Solitude is more a state of mind and heart than it is a place. There is a solitude of the heart that can be maintained at all times. Crowds, or lack of them, have little to do with this inward attentiveness. It is quite possible to be a desert hermit and never experience solitude. But if we possess inward solitude, we do not fear being alone, for we know that we are not alone.

---

[5] Henri Nouwen, *The Way of the Heart* (New York: Ballantine Books, 1981) pgs. 15-16
[6] Ibid, pg. 17

> Neither do we fear being with others, for they do not control us. In the midst of the noise and confusion, we are settled into a deep inner silence. Whether alone or among people, we always carry with us a portable sanctuary of the heart.[7]

Solitude can be unsettling, especially as we begin this journey and are not used to being alone. As soon as we get alone, it seems the battle in our minds begins raging. Henri Nouwen describes this challenge:

> As soon as I decide to stay in my solitude, confusing ideas, disturbing images, wild fantasies, and weird associations jump about in my mind like monkeys in a banana tree. Anger and greed begin to show their ugly faces. I give long, hostile speeches to my enemies and dream lustful dreams in which I am wealthy, influential, and very attractive – or poor, ugly and in need of immediate consolation…. The task is to persevere in my solitude, to stay in my cell until all my seductive visitors get tired of pounding on my door and leave me alone.[8]

Perseverance is essential. We learn to disregard the onslaught of thoughts and descend below them. Nouwen instructs,

> We enter into solitude first of all to meet our Lord and to be with Him and Him alone. Our primary task in solitude, therefore, is not to pay

---

[7] Richard Foster, *Celebration of Discipline* (San Francisco: HarperCollins, 1998) pgs. 96-97
[8] Henri Nouwen, *The Way of the Heart*, pg. 18

> undue attention to the many faces which assail us, but to keep the eyes of our mind and heart on him who is our Divine Savior.[9]

This is a significant stumbling block for many attempting contemplative prayer. As we persist, over time, we do learn to quiet our minds.

Solitude is critical for our daily prayer time, especially in the beginning. And here I do mean a purposeful separation from all others, whenever possible. As we've described, solitude can be experienced in the presence of others, but I have found my prayer is usually richer and easier when I'm physically alone.

Interior silence

Interior silence is a counterpart to solitude and equally important. Without silence, we cannot learn to discern God's voice from our own raging thoughts. He speaks where He is invited and usually in a very quiet voice that is easily dismissed. Elijah learned this lesson on Mount Sinai. The Lord did not speak in the wind, the earthquake, or the fire. Instead, He spoke to Elijah in a *still, small voice*.[10] As we grow in this relationship, we learn to discern His voice and hear more clearly.

The silence of prayer is far more than just the elimination of noise. It is an interior quiet and posture of our heart that is attentive listening. Thus, the term *interior silence*. Richard Foster clarifies this,

> Though silence involves the absence of speech, it always involves the act of listening. Simply to

---

[9] Henri Nouwen, *The Way of the Heart*, pg. 20
[10] 1 Kings 19:11-12

> refrain from talking, without a heart listening to God, is not silence. A day filled with noise and voices can be a day of silence, if the noises become for us the echo of the presence of God, if the voices are, for us, messages and solicitations of God.[11]

Similar to solitude, learning to sit in interior silence takes time. While pursuing silence, our minds can suddenly become surprisingly loud! Like solitude, however, this silence is a crucial component of contemplative prayer. In silence, we are confronted with our raging thoughts and inability to simply turn them off. We recognize the shallowness and selfishness of our interior life more clearly. His grace enables us to learn to disregard and quiet these thoughts as we grow in trust of His heart for us. This is how we nurture interior silence.

Interior silence and solitude, says Father Dubay,

> ...do not refer only to the lessening of decibels. A person, notes Teresa (*of Avila*), cannot understand the indwelling mystery and fully realize Who is present within until he closes his eyes to the vanities of this world. Were she in our midst at the end of the twentieth century, the saint would no doubt specify that this means a drastic reduction in our exposure to the mass media, especially electronic media of television, radio, and film.[12]

---

[11] Richard Foster, *Celebration of Discipline*, pg. 98
[12] Thomas Dubay, *Fire Within* (San Francisco: Ignatius Press, 1989) pg. 123, *italics mine*

The categories may be a bit outdated, but we get the point. The Holy Spirit is able to reveal the true state of our own hearts in this place of silence. This is a shocking revelation for us as we are faced with our selfishness and brokenness. We are learning, however, that we can be honest about ourselves and trust Him. In silence and stillness, we cease putting on human facades and embrace our wretchedness and nakedness[13] before a holy, loving Father. It is here that we both meet our true selves as well as the waiting Father. And it is during these interactions that He transforms and heals us.

The Holy Spirit will gently lead us in this journey towards interior silence. He knows we desire to hear Him. We should do whatever it takes to eliminate distractions that divert our attention from Him.

Centering prayer

Centering prayer is a primary exercise of contemplative prayer with the goal of learning to experience interior silence. Here, we utilize all three of the disciplines we have discussed. The following is a summary of steps for the practice of centering prayer. Catholic mystic Father Thomas Keating has several teaching videos available on YouTube that you may find helpful.[14]

It is important to reiterate that contemplative prayer is a relationship; it is not based on formulas or performance. God is moved by our desire to be with Him. It is helpful to follow guidelines like the ones

---

[13] Revelation 3:17-18
[14] Thomas Keating Centering Prayer Guidelines Intro:
   https://www.youtube.com/watch?v=3IKpFHfNdnE

below that have been developed by those who have gone before us. God will not, however, be disappointed or discipline us if we do this incorrectly. We must believe this.

The Holy Spirit is our teacher and is very capable of directing us. We can have confidence that He will correct and redirect us as necessary. Our primary job is to respond, by grace, to the persistent beckoning of the lover of our souls.

Steps for centering prayer

The first step is to purpose in your heart to set this time aside. Next, select a comfortable location and sit down. It is at this point that the Holy Spirit, enraptured in love, 'has you.' He is committed to guiding and instructing you in deep prayer with the heart of the Father.

Next, choose a sacred word or phrase as the symbol of your intention to consent to God's presence and actions within you. He will not violate your free will but responds to your invitation. In *The Way of the Heart*, Henri Nouwen summarizes instructions of the Desert Fathers for selecting a word or phrase:

> When you pray do not try to express yourself in fancy words, for often it is the simple, repetitious phrases of a little child that our Father in heaven finds most irresistible. Do not strive for verbosity lest your mind be distracted from devotion by a search for words.[15]

---

[15] Henri Nouwen, *The Way of the Heart*, pg. 80

Sitting comfortably and with eyes closed, take a deep breath, and settle yourself. Next, slowly and quietly introduce the sacred word or phrase, acknowledging His presence and giving Him permission to work in your heart. This is a loving relationship, and God can do whatever He desires. We are here in humility, for His pleasure. This is a quiet, slow conversation moving towards communion. Henri Nouwen's instruction from the Desert Fathers is helpful:

> The quiet repetition of a single word can help us to descend with the mind into the heart. This repetition has nothing to do with magic. It is not meant to throw a spell on God or to force Him into hearing us. On the contrary, a word or sentence repeated frequently can help us to concentrate, to move to the center, to create an inner stillness and thus, to listen to the voice of God.[16]

As we quiet ourselves, we will inevitably begin to encounter all sorts of distractions, thoughts, memories, and so on that will flow down our stream of consciousness. These are normal. These thoughts do not disqualify us, nor should they condemn or upset us. Remember, we are sitting in God's presence, and He is fully aware of what is in our hearts and minds. These thoughts do not disturb or trouble Him, nor should they trouble us. Like the background music in the grocery store, we put up with them but pay no attention to them. We simply let them pass us by and return ever-so-gently to the sacred word or phrase.

---

[16] Henri Nouwen, *The Way of the Heart*, pg. 81

It is important that we do not resist these thoughts but rather have a joyful attitude toward them. If we resist them or react to them negatively, our emotions and attention will be focused on these thoughts instead of learning to let them go and get beyond them. An inappropriate reaction to these thoughts can be much more harmful than just letting them go.

As we allow thoughts to pass us by, we will begin to experience a deep silence and peace. We have arrived at the center of our being and, by faith, sit quietly in stillness with our God. Distractions will come and go, and we may need to repeat our sacred phrase many times, but this is how we learn to become more comfortable in the stillness of His presence. We stay here until we feel He has ended our time together.

It is important to reiterate that settling into this place of peace and silence is solely a work of His grace. We cannot enter by an act of our will. We will not, therefore, be able to sit in this place every time we try to do so. We make room and a place for Him, but He draws us into this intimate fellowship as He desires. Through practice and perseverance, we can grow in clearing our minds and ignoring distractions. Entering into His stillness, however, is by His grace alone.

Author Joan Chittister provides a fitting summary in *Illuminated Life*:

> Prayer is a long, slow process. First, it indicates to us how far we really are from the mind of God. When the ideas are foreign to us, when the process itself is boring or meaningless, when the quiet sitting in the presence of God in the self is a waste of time, then we have not

yet begun to pray. But little by little, one gospel, one word, one moment of silence at a time, we come to know ourselves and the barriers we put between ourselves and the God who is trying to consume us.[17]

The disciplines discussed above are the essence of contemplative prayer. Sister Chittister continues:

> The contemplative is the one among us in whom prayer, deep reflection on the presence and activity of God in the self and the world, has come little by little to extinguish the illusions of autonomy and the enthronement of the self that make little kingdoms of us all. The contemplative goes beyond the self, and all its delusions, to Life itself. One prayer at a time, contemplatives allow the heart of God to beat in the heart they call their own.[18]

Allowing the heart of God to beat in us is the fruit of contemplative prayer. We grow in the life He has placed within us. This is what transforms us from the inside out so that life is forever changed.

Our part

Contemplative prayer is a work of grace; however, we do have a part to play. This is one of many paradoxes of the Christian journey. The more we sow, the more we will reap, but we cannot cause this relationship to grow. That is wholly in God's hands.

---

[17] Joan Chittister, *Illuminated Life* (New York, Maryknoll, 2003) pgs. 92-93
[18] Ibid, pg. 94

> So then neither he who plants is anything, nor he who waters, but God who gives the increase. **(1 Corinthians 3:7)**

And

> Do not be deceived, God is not mocked; for whatever a man sows, that he will also reap. For he who sows to his flesh will of the flesh reap corruption, but he who sows to the Spirit will of the Spirit reap everlasting life. And let us not grow weary while doing good, for in due season we shall reap if we do not lose heart. **(Galatians 6:7-9)**

While there are many challenges as we begin this journey, making time is likely the most difficult first step. In *Secrets of the Secret Place*, author Bob Sorge says,

> Here's the awesome secret of Galatians 6: when you sow to the Spirit by giving dedicated time to the secret place, you will eventually reap life in the Spirit. Eventually…. It is impossible to sow to the Spirit without reaping a corresponding harvest.[19]

This takes us back to Chapter 1 and the truth that God desires to be with us. When we purpose to meet with Him, He cannot stay away. Time invested in this relationship is not wasted!

Additionally, it must be reiterated that this is about a relationship. Contemplative prayer is about the journey, not arriving at an experience. I have spent hours as a slave to my mind, feeling like disconnecting

---

[19] Bob Sorge, *Secrets of the Secret Place*, pgs. 23-24

from my own thoughts will never happen; I'll never be able to contemplate like the mystics have described. And then, just for a brief moment, my thoughts cease, and His peace becomes some kind of tangible mystical substance enveloping me. In faith, we believe He is always with us, but experiencing His presence in some way is entirely His grace. It cannot be forced or rushed, nor should it be expected each time we pray.

Contemplative prayer is not just this brief encounter with the Prince of Peace. It has been the entire journey of intention to be alone with Him. This cannot be stressed enough. His grace is always at work in us, even when participating in these exercises seems hopeless.

Chapter 5 –

SEARCH MY HEART, OH GOD

Search me, O God, and know my heart; Try me, and know my anxieties; And see if there is any wicked way in me, and lead me in the way everlasting. **(Psalm 139:23-24)**

The unexamined life is not worth living. **(Socrates)**

Recently, I had a conversation with a young father about his relationship with his 5-year-old son. As with many 5-year-olds, his son wants to appear "bigger and better" than he is and has taken to telling lies. His father, of course, won't tolerate lying and spends time patiently correcting and teaching his son that lying is wrong. Correction is important, necessary, and scriptural. Dad is not angry or disappointed with his immature son. Nor does he have a desire to stop spending time with him; he loves him deeply. And he is confident his son will receive his instruction and grow out of this phase. He feels a bit sad that the time he spends with his son is sometimes spent correcting his lies. Dad knows discipline is part of his job, but time together is precious.

This experience with his immature son demonstrates another paradox of our prayer life. I believe that how we approach our time with God is important. It is wise to remember that we are meeting with the God who created the Cosmos, not placing an order at the McDonald's drive-through. At the same time, we can and need to bring our hearts before our loving Father in ANY and ALL conditions. Contemplative prayer is about learning to present ourselves before our God as we are. It is in His presence that we are transformed. We do not "clean ourselves up" in order to seek Him, but nor do we approach Him irreverently or flippantly.

As I have already written, we can't fix ourselves and need the Holy Spirit's grace. We can, however, hinder the work of the Holy Spirit and delay receiving the grace we need. We are often slow to address issues that could and should be resolved more quickly and less painfully than we allow. Sometimes out of ignorance, but other times because of our stubbornness.

As I write this chapter, the Holy Spirit is shining His light on envy and jealousy in my own life. The context is not important, but it provides an example of how we can hinder His work in our lives. The envy and jealousy I feel in my soul are nauseating. I cannot, however, by an act of my will, eliminate it from my thoughts. Now that it has been uncovered, it is there, and I'm helpless to remove it. I need His grace to eliminate this from my heart.

I find myself wanting to default to justifying these feelings and placing blame on others. And so, I have a choice. My first option is to continue entertaining these harmful thoughts and allow their poison to cloud my thoughts and rob me of joy. This is an easy, familiar option that my soul is used to. Something inside enjoys wallowing in the muck of sin. This requires that I come to God guarded, ready to justify my position that His love for me is not enough, nor are His words of truth in scripture applicable in this situation.

The second option is to bring these thoughts before the Lord in my prayer time and own them. To confess my inability to change myself, cry out for mercy, repent (express my desire to turn from these thoughts), and receive the forgiveness Jesus purchased for me on the cross. This is gospel truth, and it requires that I choose to let go of this envy and jealousy. I come to Him in humility with an aching heart, longing for transformation. This option allows Him to work more quickly and empower me to receive His grace and forgiveness and move on.

Jesus told His disciples at the last supper, *I still have many things to say to you, but you cannot bear them now* (John 16:12). I wonder how often Jesus might be saying the same thing to me? Are the hurry and anxiety in my life slowing my spiritual progress? Or is an unwillingness to let go of past hurts and offer forgiveness delaying a truth He desires to communicate to me? Or are arrogance and unwillingness to let Him be Lord in my life preventing the fulfillment of a promise?

Jesus goes on to promise the disciples (and us) that the Holy Spirit will *guide you into all truth* (John 16:12). This promise is the source of our hope and a foundational truth in our lives. Even though His grace and mercy are abundant when I'm slow to listen or fail to heed His voice, it pains me to hinder or slow His transformative work in my life. It is always beneficial to agree with the work of the Holy Spirit.

The young father's heart is a beautiful reflection of our Heavenly Father's heart. He is not mad or disappointed at the condition of our hearts and will always meet us right where we are. Time on earth is short, however, and He has much He desires to say to us.

The following are a few human struggles that are detrimental to the practice of contemplative prayer. There are many other hindrances, but these have been a particular focus of our church community and are especially challenging for me. We are unable to eliminate these from our lives by an act of our will and need help from the Holy Spirit, who is committed to transforming our hearts.

Hurry and anxiety

When reading the gospels, do you ever feel frustrated like I do that Jesus was never in a hurry or anxious? How could He live as a human without hurry and anxiety? Life without these unfortunate companions is foreign to my American way of life.

While on earth, Jesus led His life in a way that contradicts our restless human hearts. He was asleep on the rough sea when circumstances demanded immediate concern.[1] He was patient when His disciples were not getting it at the last supper.[2] He was at peace when He should have been anxious the night of His arrest, as His ministry on earth seemed to be unraveling.[3]

---

[1] Mark 4:38
[2] John 14
[3] John 18:11

In his book, *The Ruthless Elimination of Hurry*, author and pastor John Mark Comer writes,

> Hurry kills all we hold dear: spirituality, health, marriage, family, thoughtful work, creativity, generosity…name your value. Hurry is a sociopathic predator loose in our society.[4]

And in most cases, anxiety is the fuel of hurry. Hurry and anxiety will kill contemplative prayer.

In *The Shattered Lantern*, Ronald Rolheiser refers to this as unbridled restlessness.[5] This is the opposite of restfulness, which is one of our most powerful, innate cravings. Deep down, we all long for peace and rest. We usually associate these with serene images of places or circumstances that always seem out of our reach, or attainable at some future time in our lives.

Restlessness leads to discontent with our normal lives. Nothing seems to satisfy, and we are driven to obsessive activity. Life becomes an exhausting experience. The life of Jesus displayed in the gospels was very busy, and it seems He seldom had time for rest. And yet, He always seemed restful, in control, and at peace.

Consider just one example from John's gospel of how Jesus responded to stressful, difficult circumstances. One of his best friends, Lazarus, is sick and on his deathbed in the town of Bethany. We know the story well. Jesus is requested to come by Mary and Martha,

---

[4] John Mark Comer, *The Ruthless Elimination of Hurry* (Colorado Springs: Waterbrook, 2019) pg. 53

[5] Ronald Rolheiser, *The Shattered Lantern*, (New York: Crossroad Publishing, 2001) pg. 42

sisters of Lazarus. The expectation of the sisters was that Jesus would drop everything and come as quickly as possible. They knew He could and would heal their brother as he lay on his deathbed.[6] But what does Jesus do? He delays for two days.[7]

Not only was Lazarus ill, but the religious Jews in Bethany were trying to kill Jesus.[8] Jesus seems to simply ignore the disciples' concerns about the price on His head. He doesn't even acknowledge their safety concerns, and this seems to irritate Thomas.[9] It is important to note that He also clearly told the disciples that Lazarus was dead. He was preparing them for the situation they were walking into. He is always teaching and drawing His disciples into greater faith.

Both Martha and Mary expressed their disappointment at the late arrival of Jesus.[10] But He had a plan all along that none of His closest friends, the disciples, nor Martha and Mary, could comprehend. This was an opportunity for them to grow in faith and a deeper revelation of who He is. John tells us that Jesus *groaned in the spirit and was troubled when He saw Mary weeping* (John 11:33). There is no anxiety or hurry, however, in His response to the pain of the sisters or fear of the disciples.

We must also find contentment and rest in our mundane, human existence. Without this peace, we become impatient and greedy for experience. Henri

---

[6] John 11:1-3
[7] John 11:5-7
[8] John 11:8
[9] John 11:14-16
[10] John 11:20-22&32

Nouwen sums up the impact of restlessness on our contemporary lives:

> ...the great paradox of our time is that many of us are busy and bored at the same time. While our lives are full, we are unfulfilled.[11]

How many of us spend our days feeling unfulfilled? We need to bring our hurry and anxiety before God, own them, repent (desire to change), and ask for His help to eliminate these reactions from our lives. He is faithful to transform us. God is not in a hurry or anxious, and we don't have to be either.

How to wait on the Lord

Why is it so hard to wait? Hurry and anxiety make waiting a painful endeavor. I believe an appropriate posture of waiting requires practice. It is not easy, but scripture is full of teaching about waiting upon the Lord:

> Wait and hope for and expect the Lord; be brave and of good courage and let your heart be stout and enduring. Yes, wait for and hope for and expect the Lord. **(Psalm 27:14)**

> ...I will wait on, hope in and expect in Your name, for it is good, in the presence of Your saints. **(Psalm 52:9)**

> But those who wait on the Lord shall renew their strength; they shall mount up with wings

---

[11] Henri Nouwen, *Making all Things New: An Invitation to the Spiritual Life* (New York: HarperCollins, 1981) pg. 30

> like eagles, they shall run and not be weary, they shall walk and not faint. **(Isaiah 40:31)**

It is clear that God does not move according to our demands or timeline. As we've seen, He is never in a hurry. More importantly, it takes time for us to develop trust in this relationship. Faith is the virtue that enables us to trust and wait patiently for our Heavenly Father. *Now faith is the substance of things hoped for, the evidence of things not seen* (Hebrews 11:1). Paul tells us in the letter to the Philippians, *And my God shall supply all your need according to His riches in glory by Christ Jesus* (Philippians 4:19). Patience is a fruit of faith and, ultimately, trust that Jesus is in control.

It seems like a silly question, but how do we wait? The answer is with anticipation! As we began practicing contemplative prayer in our church body many years ago, our pastor frequently encouraged us that waiting on God was essential and active. His words still ring true today:

> Waiting is not drifting into day dreaming. It demands keen attention, an alert mind. Waiting is silent love. Waiting says, "I love you." Waiting is wordless worship. It is not necessarily a time of listening, certainly not petitioning. It's the elevation of the mind to God. *Set your mind on things above, not on things on the earth.* **(Colossians 3:2)**[12]

Waiting demands keen attention, an alert mind! These words contain the truth of a correct posture towards

---

[12] Personal notes from Vineyard Christian Fellowship church service, January 21, 2010

our God. As we learn to wait expectantly and attentively, we are exercising patience and investing in a hope that is lasting.

Narcissism and pragmatism

In *The Shattered Lantern*, Ronald Rolheiser identifies two human struggles that keep us from experiencing the depths of contemplative prayer: narcissism and pragmatism. In defining these human conditions, Rolheiser identifies our primary struggles to make this relationship a priority. A summary is provided below.[13]

Narcissism, an excessive self-preoccupation, results in self-centeredness that hinders our ability to prefer others to ourselves. It causes us to turn inward and redefine a successful life as one that elevates individualism, selfishness, and excessive privacy as virtues. These are clearly contradictory to the life Jesus demonstrated while on earth, as well as His instruction that we must lose our lives in order to find them.

Pragmatism, a philosophy and a way of life that asserts that the truth of an idea lies in its practical efficacy, drives us to define success as that which works. Therefore, what works is the truth. While this ideal is not all bad and has resulted in many helpful things in our modern world, such as medicine, travel, technology and communications, there are also negative effects. We tend to define ourselves by what we accomplish as opposed to who we are. Doing accounts for everything. The idea of resting in God's love for us is foreign unless we earn His gaze through our accomplishments. We have little patience for the impractical use of our time.

---

[13] Ronald Rolheiser, *The Shattered Lantern*, pgs. 28 (paraphrased)

For example, it pains us to sit before a God we cannot see or hear as we begin contemplative prayer with little tangible benefit. Pragmatism robs us of the patience necessary to cultivate a deep prayer relationship with Jesus.

We all struggle with these characteristics to some degree and need to recognize their impact on our lives. We must bring these before the Lord in order to allow Him to purge all that would hinder a deeper relationship with Him. He'll bring us to the place where His love compels us and we trust His perfect plan is always at work in our lives. Narcissism will be replaced with a heart of charity, and pragmatism with patient obedience.

Chapter 6

POSTURES OF THE HEART

Above all else, guard your heart, for everything you do flows from it. **(Proverbs 4:23 NIV)**

A good man out of the good treasure of his heart brings forth good; and an evil man out of the evil treasure of his heart brings forth evil. For out of the abundance of the heart his mouth speaks. **(Luke 6:45)**

In the last chapter, we looked at some characteristics that are detrimental to contemplative prayer. The following are additional considerations as we enter our prayer time. I refer to these as *postures[1] of the heart*. While there are many more ways to take inventory of the heart, these have been important to me. Growing in and practicing these postures are beneficial to our prayer life. They are in no particular order.

---

[1] Posture: a conscious mental or outward behavioral attitude. (Merriam-Webster Dictionary)

Humility before God

Scripture is very clear that the proud have no place before God. It is quite a remarkable thought that the God of the universe is drawn to the humble[2] and lowly.

Scripture clearly portrays the Lord's thoughts regarding the humble, and the opposite, the proud:

> The fear of the Lord is the instruction of wisdom, and before honor is humility. **(Proverbs 15:33)**
>
> Though the Lord is on high, Yet He regards the lowly; But the proud He knows from afar. **(Psalm 138:6)**
>
> Humble yourselves in the sight of the Lord, and He will lift you up. **(James 4:10)**
>
> For whoever exalts himself will be humbled, and he who humbles himself will be exalted. **(Luke 14:11)**

Bob Sorge clearly identifies humility as necessary to nurture our prayer life,

> Our violent pursuit of God must be wedded to a gentle and humble spirit. Humility is the foundation of all prayer…Prayerlessness is the first sign of prideful independence.[3]

---

[2] Humble: not proud or haughty: not arrogant or assertive; reflecting, expressing, or offered in a spirit of deference or submission. (Merriam-Webster Dictionary)

[3] Bob Sorge, *Secrets of the Secret Place*, (Grandview: Oasis House, 2018) pg. 46

He goes on to remind us that embracing humility leads to Godly riches,

> He is everything, and as we are joined to Him, the poverty of our personal identity is lost in the fullness of His eternal greatness...God dignifies us – with sonship, glory, acceptance, royalty, purpose, significance, wealth, honor, salvation, wisdom, revelation, understanding, status, character, holiness, victories – so that we might enjoy the highest privilege of casting it all at His feet. What a holy privilege is ours, to come into the throne room of His presence and empty ourselves of all dignity by prostrating ourselves before Him, worshiping Him with our entire being.[4]

Perhaps what is most amazing is that we don't always approach God in humility. The arrogance of a created being carrying pride before the Creator is unfathomable. And yet, how often do we fail to give Him the honor due Him? David's words in Psalm 145:8 cannot be overstated, *The Lord is gracious and full of compassion, Slow to anger and great in mercy.*

Humility towards one another

Humility towards one another is equally important in God's holy government. How we treat one another directly impacts our relationship with Jesus. He made a startling remark to the disciples regarding who would be the greatest in the Kingdom of God:

---

[4] Bob Sorge, *Secrets of the Secret Place*, pg. 47

His Constant Call

> At that time the disciples came to Jesus, saying, "Who then is greatest in the kingdom of heaven?" Then Jesus called a little child to Him, set him in the midst of them, and said, "Assuredly, I say to you, unless you are converted and become as little children, you will by no means enter the kingdom of heaven. Therefore whoever humbles himself as this little child is the greatest in the kingdom of heaven. **(Matthew 18:1-4)**

Intelligence, power, strength, and communication skills were not criteria.

Jesus practiced the humility that He preached during His time on earth. His entire life was an obedient response to His Father's heart for humanity. *For God so loved the world that He gave His only begotten Son.*[5]

Of course, the ultimate act of humility was His willingness to go to the cross for us. *Greater love has no one than this, than to lay down one's life for his friends.* **(John 3:16)**

Peter and Paul carried on the instructions of Jesus:

> Yes, all of you be submissive to one another, and be clothed with humility, for "God resists the proud, but gives grace to the humble." **(1 Peter 5:5)**

Humility towards others is a posture we learn, not something we're born with. In His kindness and grace, the Lord provides ample opportunity to exercise these spiritual muscles. We can all think of many situations

---

[5] John 3:16

throughout the day to heed Paul's instruction to the Philippians,

> Let nothing be done through selfish ambition or conceit, but in lowliness of mind let each esteem others better than himself. Let each of you look out not only for his own interests, but also for the interests of others. **(Philippians 2:3-4)**

As we consciously defer to and esteem one another, humility will grow within us.

Forgiveness

Jesus said some staggering things about forgiveness. We know He came to earth to purchase forgiveness for our sins. John, among other New Testament authors, makes this clear:

> And He [that same Jesus] is the propitiation for our sins [the atoning sacrifice that holds back the wrath of God that would otherwise be directed at us because of our sinful nature—our worldliness, our lifestyle]; and not for ours alone, but also for [the sins of all believers throughout] the whole world. **(1 John 2:2 AMP)**

Forgiveness is at the foundation of our Christian faith. Jesus gave the ultimate sacrifice so that you and I can be made clean before God. This created the way for intimacy with a holy Creator. We are called to forgive others as we have been forgiven,

> And forgive us our debts, as we forgive our debtors...For if you forgive men their trespasses, your heavenly Father will also

> forgive you. But if you do not forgive men their trespasses, neither will your Father forgive your trespasses. **(Matthew 6:12 & 14-15)**

This was obviously a very important truth that Jesus emphasized several times throughout the gospels. He was clear about His expectations for His followers and the consequences of disobedience,

> And when you stand praying, if you hold anything against anyone, forgive him, that your Father in heaven may also forgive you your trespasses. But if you do not forgive, neither will your Father in heaven forgive your trespasses. **(Mark 11:25-26)**

Paul and John reiterate the teachings of Jesus regarding forgiveness,

> Therefore, as the elect of God, holy and beloved, put on tender mercies, kindness, humility, meekness, longsuffering; bearing with one another, and forgiving one another, if anyone has a complaint against another; even as Christ forgave you, so you also must do. **(Colossians 3:12-13)**

> If we confess our sins, He is faithful and just to forgive us our sins and to cleanse us from all unrighteousness. **(1 John 1:9)**

The Holy Spirit will not allow us to sit quietly very long with unforgiveness in our hearts. We must learn to be quick recipients of God's forgiveness for our own sins. Equally important, we must be quick to forgive others.

Repentance

Repentance is a change of the attitude of the heart that turns from sin towards God. It is breaking our agreement with darkness and agreeing with God and His ways. We change our behavior and actions based on the truth we have received.

Jesus paid the price for our sin so that we can come before God in confidence that we won't be rejected. His work on the cross, the resurrection, and His ascension were complete and final. All we have to do is believe and accept it. As Paul instructs us,

> ...for all have sinned and fall short of the glory of God, being justified freely by His grace through the redemption that is in Christ Jesus, whom God set forth as a propitiation by His blood, through faith, to demonstrate His righteousness, because in His forbearance God had passed over the sins that were previously committed, to demonstrate at the present time His righteousness, that He might be just and the justifier of the one who has faith in Jesus. **(Romans 3:23-26)**

Faith in God's mercy gives us confidence that we can have a new beginning with God after we repent, that our sin is no longer before him. As David says in Psalm 103:12, *As far as the east is from the west, so far has He removed our transgressions (sins) from us.* What a life-transforming truth.

Even when our genuine repentance doesn't seem to last long and we find ourselves sinning once again, God knows the intention of our weak hearts. That's what moves Him, not the success of our battle with sin. Of course, we will eventually win as we grow and mature in His love for us, but even in our weakness and immaturity, He receives our honest repentance as real.

Bob Sorge has some great advice that I wholeheartedly agree with,

> …Become a good repenter. The only way to move forward in God is through repentance. If your pride hinders you from repenting, get over it. You're a wretch. You need mercy so badly it's scary. Wise up and master the art of repentance. Call your sin in its worst possible terms. Grovel. Eat Dust.[6]

His advice is worth emphasizing again. Repent quickly and move on! Wallowing in our sin and refusing to repent and receive forgiveness is the ultimate act of heresy and a prideful heart. It says that what Jesus accomplished on the cross wasn't enough for my sin, or the sins of others against me.

Author Calvin Miller has some instruction for us regarding overcoming sin, which is one of the transformational fruits of contemplative prayer. We cannot change ourselves, but we can be transformed as we behold our Savior.

> The best way, then, to deal with sin is not to attempt reform but to adore the Savior. Winning over our lower nature is made positive by adoration. While we worship the enthroned

---

[6] Bob Sorge, *Secrets of the Secret Place*, pgs.19-20

and inner Christ, we cannot be intrigued by negative preoccupations with sin.[7]

Persistence[8]

In Luke 11:5-8, Jesus tells a parable of a man whose friend arrives in the middle of the night. The man has nothing to offer his travel-weary friend, so he goes to his neighbor. He knocks on the door to ask his neighbor for food, but his neighbor essentially tells him that it's late, he's in bed, and to go away. But the man keeps knocking and knocking. The neighbor finally gets up and gives him what he wants in order to get rid of him. Jesus then explains the meaning of the parable:

> I say to you, though he will not rise and give to him because he is his friend, yet because of his persistence he will rise and give him as many as he needs. "So I say to you, ask, and it will be given to you; seek, and you will find; knock, and it will be opened to you. For everyone who asks receives, and he who seeks finds, and to him who knocks it will be opened." **(Luke 11:8-10)**

At least one message is that our Father desires us to ask and rewards persistence. This should greatly encourage us. Of course, the flip side of that coin is that this relationship takes time and *requires* persistence. We need to settle in our hearts that we are in this for the long term. The unknown author of *The Cloud of Unknowing* puts it this way,

---

[7] Calvin Miller, *Table of Inwardness* (Downers Grove: Inter-Varsity Press, 1984) pg. 29

[8] Persist - to go on resolutely or stubbornly in spite of opposition, importunity, or warning. (Merriam-Webster Dictionary)

> For I tell you frankly that anyone who really desires to be a contemplative will know the pain of arduous toil (unless God should intervene with special grace); he will feel keenly the cost of constant effort until he is long accustomed to this work...But persevere in doing your part and I promise you that God will not fail to do His.[9]

Missionary Dr. Frank Laubach clearly summarizes the expectations of a relationship with our Lord in *Letters by a Modern Mystic*:

> We shall not become like Christ until we give Him more time. A teacher's college requires students to attend classes for twenty-five hours a week for three years. Could it prepare competent teachers or a law school prepare competent lawyers if they studied only ten minutes a week? Neither can Christ, and He never pretended that He could. To His disciples, He said: "Come with me, walk with me, talk and listen to me, work and rest with me, eat and sleep with me, twenty-four hours a day for three years."[10]

By faith, we believe that God leads us at the pace He determines is best for us. He desires a relationship above all and is committed to us for the long haul: eternity. We will spend eternity learning about His

---

[9] Author unknown, *The Cloud of Unknowing* (New York: Random House, 1973) pg. 73

[10] Frank C. Laubach, *Letters by a Modern Mystic* (Colorado Springs: Purposeful Design Publications, 2007) pg. 88

goodness and enjoying Him. Persistence in this life will bring a reward in the next.

Obedience

The idea of practicing obedience to God makes some of us tremble. We immediately think about all the things we don't want to do or that scare us. We believe God will try to test us in terrifying ways. This is a wrong idea of His heart and plans for our lives. Although He does require obedience as we grow in relationship with Him, we can trust His guidance and direction.

God desires (and requires) obedience in order to deepen our trust in Him. Maturity in faith, I believe, allows us to walk more like Him. He doesn't require obedience just to jerk us around. He has greater things to give us that we can't handle until we learn to trust Him. We must believe Paul's exhortation to the church at Ephesus:

> For we are His workmanship [His own master work, a work of art], created in Christ Jesus [reborn from above—spiritually transformed, renewed, ready to be used] for good works, which God prepared [for us] beforehand [taking paths which He set], so that we would walk in them [living the good life which He prearranged and made ready for us]. **(Ephesians 2:10 AMP)**

We can trust God's plan for our lives, no matter how confusing it may seem at times. Paul tells the church at Ephesus (and us) that God's plans for us are far greater than we can imagine:

> Now to Him who is able to [carry out His purpose and] do superabundantly more than all that we dare ask or think [infinitely beyond our greatest prayers, hopes, or dreams], according to His power that is at work within us... **(Ephesians 3:20 AMP)**

Sorge sums this up,

> Hearing God in the secret place is one of the greatest keys to the overcoming Christian life. However, it must be linked with its corollary: radical obedience. We hear, and then we do. *"But be doers of the word, and not hearers only, deceiving yourselves."* **(James 1:22)"**[11]

He goes on to emphasize that our obedience begins with a relationship:

> Implicit obedience starts, for every one of us, not in doing good works but in sitting at His feet and hearing His word. Devotion to the secret place is the saint's first great act of obedience...The true fulfillment of serving Jesus is discovered when we get first things first: First we sit and listen, and then we go and do.[12]

We must learn to obey His voice in order to grow in a relationship with Him. This is non-negotiable. The more we grow in our relationship with God and learn to trust Him, the more obedient we will become.

---

[11] Bob Sorge, *Secrets of the Secret Place*, pg. 14
[12] Ibid, pgs. 14&15

Gratitude

A spirit of gratitude may be the most important posture of the human heart. If we understood more fully what Jesus accomplished for us, gratitude would be the only logical response. Paul exhorts the Thessalonians,

> Rejoice always, pray without ceasing, in everything give thanks; for this is the will of God in Christ Jesus for you. **(1 Thessalonians 5:16-17)**

Father Rolheiser sums it up well,

> To be a saint is to be motivated by gratitude, nothing more and nothing less. In the end, gratitude is the root of all virtue. It lies at the base of love and charity. Scripture always and everywhere makes this point.[13]

He goes on,

> To be a saint is never to take anything as owed, but to receive everything, gratefully, as gift. Proper receptivity and gratitude lie at the root of purity of heart. They are the real beatitudes. Matthew 5:8 could just as easily be rendered: "Blessed are those who are grateful, who see and appreciate everything as a gift, for they shall see god."[14]

We have likely all experienced the joy of giving a gift that is received with joy, and more importantly, enjoyed by the recipient. Children are especially good at

---

[13] Ronald Rolheiser, *The Shattered Lantern*, pg. 180
[14] Ibid, pg. 182

receiving and enjoying good gifts. That really is the greatest compliment the giver of the gift can receive. How much more is God moved when His children receive His good gifts and enjoy them. It's a staggering thought that we can bring the Creator pleasure by simply enjoying His creation and gifts in our lives. He is so deserving of all our gratitude!

Chapter 7

NURTURING A PRAYER LIFE: SOME PRACTICAL CONSIDERATIONS

…in our attempts to understand how God speaks to us and guides us we must, above all, hold on to the fact that learning how to hear God is to be sought only as part of a certain kind of life, a life of loving fellowship with the King and his other subjects within the kingdom of the heavens. We must never forget that God's speaking to us is intended to develop into an intelligent, freely cooperative relationship between mature people who love each other with the richness of genuine agape love.[1]

…I carry out my actions with the desire to please the Lord and then let all else come as it will.[2]

How can we create a space for and nurture a prayer life in our fast-paced, busy lives? It has been our experience that the practice of contemplative prayer is born out of

---

[1] Dallas Willard, *Hearing God* (Downers Grove: Intervarsity Press, 2012) pg. 39
[2] Brother Lawrence & Frank Laubach, *Practicing His Presence* (Jacksonville: SeedSowers Publishing, 1973) pg. 48

a commitment to a consistent prayer life. Without a habitual, established time alone with God, contemplative prayer will be challenging.

It's worth repeating here that we are not talking about a regimented time of prayer that we should feel guilty about missing. That's not the point of a loving relationship with our Lord. A commitment is required to prioritize this relationship, but we do our best through difficult seasons of life that may require attention and energy to be placed elsewhere, especially with kids. God is not keeping track of the time we spend with Him or disappointed when we are unable to spend the time we desire. Our busy days are full of opportunities to dialogue with Him as He is with us always. The desire and intention of our hearts, I believe, are more important than the time spent with Him.

The following are a few practical considerations when establishing a prayer life that leads to contemplative prayer. I've highlighted just a few key issues from my own experience, but I know there are many more. These are in no particular order.

Forming good habits

Creating good habits takes purposeful, hard work, and we often struggle until they become a part of our lives. In order to make a change, we begin with an act of our will. Developing a daily prayer life is no different. While this relationship is a work of God's grace, we must begin with an act of our will, with a decision. And while He is constantly drawing us to Himself, we persevere through determination. Once a habit begins to form, it must become a lifestyle for the practice to be lasting. Our prayer life is similar to physical exercise in this

His Constant Call

sense. Physical exercise is most beneficial when it becomes part of our daily routine. It's then that we stop worrying so much about results.

Frank Laubach says it this way,

> You will find this just as easy and just as hard as forming any other habit. You have hitherto thought of God for only a few seconds or minutes a week, and He was out of your mind the rest of the time. Now you are attempting, like Brother Lawrence, to have God in mind each minute you are awake. Such a drastic change in habit requires a real effort at the beginning.[3]

Forming a habit, however, is only the first step in this journey. Working towards establishing the habit of spending time with our Lord must lead to something more. My experience has been that what began as a habit transformed into a desire and has now become a necessity, and the most important part of my day. Oswald Chamber's guidance is very helpful:

> When we first begin to form a habit, we are fully aware of it. There are times when we are aware of becoming virtuous and godly, but this awareness should only be a stage we quickly pass through as we grow spiritually. If we stop at this stage, we will develop a sense of spiritual pride. The right thing to do with godly habits is to immerse them in the life of the Lord until

---

[3] Frank Laubach, *Letters by a Modern Mystic* (Colorado Springs: Purposeful Design, 2007) pg. 92

they become such a spontaneous expression of our lives that we are no longer aware of them.[4]

How Jesus transforms this time set aside with Him will surprise you. One day, you'll forget the difficulty of making time for Him and realize that your days are filled with His presence in a way you could not have imagined.

First thing in the morning

For most of us, the morning presents the best opportunity for a consistent prayer time. It sets the tone for the entire day as we turn our hearts to Him when we awake. It's also the time of day when we are likely the least distracted.

Bob Sorge says it beautifully,

> Jesus' commitment to the secret place was profoundly prophesied by David in Psalm 110:3, *"In the beauties of holiness, from the womb of the morning, You have the dew of Your youth."* The secret place was Jesus' "womb of the morning." It was the place where life incubated, where creativity germinated, where inspiration gestated, where power percolated.[5]

Most important, however, is that we give God our best time of the day – whatever that is. For me personally, morning is by far the best time of the day. Those who

---

[4] Oswald Chambers, *My Utmost for His Highest*, Updated Edition (Grand Rapids: Our Daily Bread Publishing, 1992) May 12th entry

[5] Bob Sorge, *Secrets of the Secret Place* (Grandview: Oasis House, 2018) pg. 91

seek God early in the morning are not earning extra points with God. My experience, however, is that if I don't get myself out of bed and seek Him first, it becomes more difficult to seek Him later in the day. The cares of the world seem to pile up over the course of a busy day and make contemplative prayer more challenging. I find my mind is less cluttered early in the morning.

David and Isaiah speak of seeking God early[6],

> O God, You are my God; early will I seek You **(Psalm 63:1)**
>
> With my soul I have desired You in the night, yes, by my spirit within me I will seek You early… **(Isaiah 26:9)**

Jesus also demonstrates the importance of seeking the Father early. After ministering all night, He still leaves early in the morning to seek His Father alone.

> Now in the morning, having risen a long while before daylight, He (Jesus) went out and departed to a solitary place; and there He prayed. **(Mark 1:35)**

Whether morning, evening, or night, give God your best time! That's what matters most.

Kids

My wife and I had four young kids as we began this journey of contemplative prayer more than two decades ago. The oldest was 12 and the youngest 6. We also both had full-time jobs that were stressful and

---

[6] See also Psalm 5:3; Psalm 108:2 AMP

demanding. Our days were full of work, school, sports, and all the things that make life with kids wonderfully chaotic. When challenged to set an hour per day to seek God and practice contemplative prayer, we were confronted with the reality of our already full lives. We want to dedicate time, but how can we possibly do this?

As we evaluated our days, we realized that there was, in fact, time that could be made if we were willing to change some things.

The primary change for me was to try to get to bed earlier so I could set the alarm an hour earlier than usual. Our daily offering was imperfect, and we were tired most of the time, as parents are. I recall being frustrated that I couldn't devote the time I desired, but was repeatedly reassured by our pastor and others on the same path, that God was pleased with what we were able to offer Him. The intention and desire were really most important.

There is no doubt in my mind that even the weak attempts resulted in a deepening relationship with Jesus that positively impacted all of our family dynamics. Believe me, we didn't do things perfectly; most of the time, not even well. In later years, as the kids grew and moved on with their own lives, and we finally had more time; we were both shocked at how that initial desire and weak commitment had become a foundational part of our lives.

We also tried to lead our kids into contemplative prayer as we felt they were able. Our strategy was to get them up early, bring them into the living room where we could see them, and they could get comfortable. We would then put on quiet instrumental music for 30 minutes and encourage them to ask the Holy Spirit to help them quiet their hearts and minds. Sure, most of the time they fell right back to sleep, but that's ok. They were sleeping in the arms of their Father, and that's fine by me! After 30 minutes or so, we would get them up and have breakfast together. They would then get ready for school.

We also had many conversations about what we were trying to do during this prayer time of quiet. Contemplative prayer was an entirely new concept for us, but we did our best to communicate what we were learning with our kids.

I honestly don't remember when we started this with the kids or how often we got them up. My guess is that it probably didn't happen very often, but we did try. I laugh when thinking about our attempts to introduce them to contemplative prayer, but the memories are good. We followed our hearts and His call the best we could.

I am encouraged by Zechariah 4:10 (AMP), *Who [with reason] despises the day of small things (beginnings)?* These were small beginnings.

Our church community was also committed to teaching the kids how to practice silent prayer. Sunday school classes began with 5-10 minutes of silence with instruction about how to quiet their hearts, turn their attention to Jesus, and listen for the voice of God. These practice times together were important and surely impacted our kids in a positive way.

Walking

> And they heard the sound of the Lord God walking in the garden… **(Genesis 3:8)**

And,

> Enoch walked with God…and then was no more! **(Genesis 5:24)**

From the beginning, humans have walked with God! From the Garden of Eden to the shores of the Sea of Galilee to the road to Emmaus, scripture tells us that humans have walked alongside and talked with God! What a remarkable image of the Creator's desire to be with humanity. Of course, walking is a great exercise and should be part of a healthy lifestyle. It's also helpful to wake yourself up in the morning, especially in the fall or winter. Most of all, it's a great way to spend time with Jesus.

I don't walk for exercise, but I do frequently ride a bike. My bike rides have become one of the highlights of my day because it is time spent talking with the Lord. I ask Jesus to ride with me as I leave my driveway and begin an ongoing dialogue.

Walking or riding requires our minds to be engaged, paying attention to our surroundings, and making decisions about our progress. I would never discourage anyone from spending time with Jesus, but I must clarify that this is not contemplative prayer based upon my previous definition.

During contemplative prayer, we disconnect or turn off our thoughts and sit peacefully with our Savior. We need time to just sit with him in a posture that allows us not to look, listen, or make any conscious decisions.

This would be challenging while walking or participating in some other type of physical activity. One way to spend time with Jesus is not better than the other; just different. Our relationship with the Holy Trinity includes all of these types of interaction and prayer.

Praying in the Spirit

My intention below is not to present a thorough theological argument one way or the other regarding praying in the spirit (or speaking in unknown tongues). Rather, I'm sharing my own experience and that of our church community. Praying in the Spirit has been encouraged and an important part of our prayer lives in our church for decades. We believe this New Testament gift can be part of every believer's relationship with God. It can also assist us to quiet our minds and enter into contemplative prayer.

Paul's ministry and pastoral letters provide the majority of instruction regarding tongues and praying in the Spirit.

He clearly was a proponent of praying in the Spirit and believed that this prayer edifies or builds up the one praying. Paul also delineated between praying when alone versus praying in a place with others present. While speaking in tongues edifies the individual, it is meaningless in a church or group setting unless someone interprets the tongue. Paul emphasized this in letters to both the Corinthian[7] and Roman[8] churches.

---

[7] 1 Corinthians 14:2-19
[8] Romans 12:4-8

Paul says, *I thank my God I speak with tongues more than you all* (1 Corinthians 14:18). But his instruction in verse 19 is poignant:

> …yet in the church I would rather speak five words with my understanding, that I may teach others also, than ten thousand words in a tongue. **(1 Corinthians 14:19)**

He clearly speaks in tongues often when he is alone, but would rather pray with understanding in a corporate setting in order for everyone to be edified.

I have been encouraged and pastored that praying in the Spirit is a wonderful way to engage in prayer. When we don't know what to pray, we can loosen our tongues and let the Holy Spirit intercede for us. I do have a prayer language that I do not understand, and this is an important type of prayer for me personally. More frequently, however, I am aware of an internal crying out that is manifested by a handful of short statements of request or adoration that I do understand. Phrases like "Help me, Jesus," or "I praise You, Holy God" emerge from deep within me throughout much of my day. I believe this is the Holy Spirit praying in me and through me. This regular internal dialogue, along with tongues we do not understand, is part of the Holy Spirit's intercession for us.

> Likewise the Spirit also helps in our weaknesses. For we do not know what we should pray for as we ought, but the Spirit Himself makes intercession for us with groanings which cannot be uttered. Now He who searches the hearts knows what the mind of the Spirit is, because He

makes intercession for the saints according to the will of God. **(Romans 8:26-27)**

Praying in the Spirit, similar to meditation, can be an avenue into contemplative prayer. We can actively pray and then allow these prayers to quiet our souls. Pray as you are led and give the Holy Spirit permission to do what He pleases in your prayer life.

Use your imagination

We are all unique in the way we think, process information, and communicate. Our perspectives and giftings are what make us individuals. Our human tendency is to assume everyone thinks and responds the way we do. Maybe it's the pride and arrogance of the fall that makes it so difficult to recognize and appreciate the perspective of others. Some may find this section helpful, while others may find it challenging. Regardless of where you are on the imagination spectrum, this is a discussion that should be had with the Holy Spirit. He will direct and guide your prayer life.

Calvin Miller writes,

> One door opens to the world of the spirit: imagination. God's realities start at the threshold of our senses. But they go far beyond sight, smell, and sound. That is why we often miss Him altogether. To follow Christ, we must create in our minds God's unseen world, or never confront it at all.[9]

---

[9] Calvin Miller, *The Table of Inwardness* (Downers Grove: Intervarsity Press, 1984) pg. 93

His Constant Call

He goes on,

> Each of us imagines differently. Our inner visions are shaped by the world we live in. In Sunday school, black children tend to draw Black Saviors and white children, Caucasian Christs. And it is not just children. Even as grown men and women, we tend to see Christ rather like ourselves. Still, imagination stands at the front of our relationship with Christ. We cannot commune with a Savior whose form and shape elude us.[10]

I've already shared my own experience with imagination, and we've also discussed the thoughts and imagination of the poetic John of the Cross and his dark nights. Teresa of Avila is another mystic who has developed a castle metaphor to communicate the work of the Holy Spirit in our lives. Like John, her words, while challenging, are full of wisdom. The point here is that the Holy Spirit used her imagination to help her communicate His work in her life.

> I began to think of the soul as if it were a castle made of a single diamond or of very clear crystal, in which there are many rooms, just as in Heaven there are many mansions. Now if we think carefully over this, sisters, the soul of the righteous man is nothing but a paradise, in which as God tells us, He takes His delight. For what do you think a room will be like which is

---

[10] Calvin Miller, *The Table of Inwardness*, Pgs. 93-94

> the delight of a King so mighty, so wise, so pure and so full of all that is good?[11]

As with everything we do in our pursuit of God, there is always a counterfeit and danger of going astray if we lean on our own understanding. Additionally, our Lord will not allow us to get into a routine or become dependent upon techniques or processes to interact with Him. He grows our faith by forcing us to continually change how we interact with Him. Unfortunately, I'm usually slow to recognize when He is drawing me to something deeper or different. I linger too long in what may have been working even after He no longer meets with me in that way. I have certainly been corrected as I've leaned too much on imagination and emotion as signs of His presence. The Holy Spirit, however, is always faithful to lead us back to the path and correct us when we go astray.

Breathing

Controlling our breathing can be very helpful as we still our minds. It can help us quiet ourselves, relax, and reduce our heart rate. I often take a couple of long, deep breaths to begin my prayer time and settle myself.

Repeating short phrases of scripture to the rhythm of our breathing is helpful to consciously quiet our minds and hearts. For example, using His name or another very short phrase: inhale and say, "Je" and exhale and complete, "sus." Inhale and say, "Holy", exhale and say, "God."

---

[11] St. Teresa of Avila, *Interior Castle* (Mineola: Dover Publications, Inc., 2007) pg. 15

Retreat

Taking time for a retreat is an important activity in our hectic lives. Getting away to focus on silence and solitude can help us de-clutter our minds and hearts and reset our life priorities. In *Invitation to Retreat*, author Ruth Haley Barton describes retreat:

> Retreat in the context of the spiritual life is an *extended time apart* for the purpose of being with God and giving God our full and undivided attention; it is, as Emilie Griffin puts it, "a generous commitment to our friendship with God." The emphasis is on the words *extended* and *generous*. Truth is, we are not always generous with ourselves where God is concerned.[12]

"A generous commitment to our friendship with God" is a challenging concept. We desire to be generous, especially with our time, but the idea of retreat - spending extended time alone with God - terrifies most of us. While at the same time, there is a deep longing within us that desires time to unwind, decompress, forget the cares of the world, and give ourselves completely to our Lord. The thought of retreat resonates deeply with us.

The New Testament provides examples of disconnecting from life's demands to be with God. It is clear from all four gospels that Jesus and His disciples regularly

---

[12] Ruth Haley Barton, *Invitation to Retreat* (Downers Grove: InterVarsity Press, 2018) pgs. 4-5

retreated from the masses, taking time weekly to be with one another and celebrate God's goodness.

An example occurs in the Gospel of Mark after Jesus sent out the 12 disciples in groups of two. Before sending them, He empowered them to cast out unclean spirits and share the gospel. Upon their return, they were excited to tell Jesus about all they had experienced. Jesus recognized their need to get away from the crowds and just be alone with Him,

> And He said to them, "Come aside by yourselves to a deserted place and rest a while." For there were many coming and going, and they did not even have time to eat. So they departed to a deserted place in the boat by themselves. **(Mark 6:31-32)**

He knows when we need to get away with Him and will gently draw us. I've taken a few 3-day retreats and they have been very worthwhile. While challenging at the start to decompress and unplug, Jesus has been faithful to meet me. I spend time walking, meditating, reading, and writing. He has met me in more subtle ways than I've expected, but I've always left feeling like He's been close to me. Ruth Haley Barton presents us with a challenge:

> The yearning for retreat: Can you feel it? That yearning is your invitation. It is the Spirit of God stirring up your deepest longings and questions in order to draw you deeper into the intimacy with the God you were created for.[13]

---

[13] Ruth Haley Barton, *Invitation to Retreat*, Pg. 6

Chapter 8

A Long Obedience in the Same Direction

The essential thing 'in heaven and earth' is...that there should be long obedience in the same direction; there thereby results, and has always resulted in the long run, something which has made life worth living.[1]

Eugene Peterson used the quote above from the philosopher, Friedrich Nietzsche, to title his book about the Songs of Ascent, or Psalms 120-134, *A Long Obedience in the Same Direction*. Peterson says, *"It is this 'long obedience in the same direction' which the mood of the world does so much to discourage."*[2] Nietzsche penned this in the late 19th century, and Peterson wrote his book in 1980. It's amazing how both their words still ring true today.

Our culture does everything in its power to keep us thinking in the "here and now." It loudly proclaims, "We not only need, but deserve satisfaction and pleasure right now!" And it guarantees that society has

---

[1] Friedrich Nietzsche, quoted by Eugene Peterson, *A Long Obedience in the Same Direction* (Downers Grove: InterVarsity Press) pg. 17
[2] Ibid, pg. 17

just what is required to meet those perceived needs, just point and click. I'm reminded of the scene from the 1971 movie of *Willie Wonka & the Chocolate Factory* when Veruka Salt sees the geese that lay the golden eggs full of chocolate and cries, "Daddy, I want one now!" Obtaining those things that require long-term commitment is almost a thing of the past as our culture emphasizes instant and entitled gratification. Of course, there are some who recognize the need for long-term discipline in order to meet goals. But many of us constantly seek instant gratification with little vision for the benefits of long-term commitment.

Peterson goes on,

> We assume that if something can be done at all, it can be done quickly and efficiently. Our attention spans have been conditioned by thirty-second commercials. Our sense of reality has been flattened by thirty-page abridgements. It is not difficult in such a world to get a person interested in the message of the gospel; it is terrifically difficult to sustain the interest.[3]

Peterson's observations are heartbreaking, but I believe they are correct. In our fast-paced, satisfaction-now culture, the demand for spiritual encounters and experiences likely exceeds the patience required for a long-term spiritual life of transformation. Peterson goes on:

> There is a great market for religious experience in our world, there is little enthusiasm for the patient acquisition of virtues, little inclination

---

[3] Eugene Peterson, *A Long Obedience in the Same Direction*, pg. 16

to sign up for a long apprenticeship in what earlier generations of Christians called holiness.[4]

A long obedience in the same direction, I believe, is part of God's perfect plan to bring maturity to His church. It is a paradox of this journey to embrace settling in for the long run while also learning to daily receive His blessings and mercies that are new each morning.[5] We are not deferring our hope until a later day, but rather, learning to receive all He has for us by faith every day. We also recognize that we are growing in a deeper relationship and understanding that leads to experiencing more of Him.

Identity crisis

I met Jesus through a supernatural encounter in Munich, Germany, when I was 22yearsold. My world was turned upside-down when, for the first time in my life, I experienced redemption and forgiveness, and a sense of being clean before God. It truly was a rebirth. The world was suddenly fresh and holy and full of wonder. At the same time, new questions about my identity were raised. Was I still the same person as prior to this encounter? Or was I someone completely new? So, I began my journey to discover this new identity in Christ.

There are many scriptures highlighting the newness of life when we accept Jesus as our Lord and Savior. These beautiful truths about our new identity in Christ are foundational to the Christian faith. They are also quite

---

[4] Eugene Peterson, *A Long Obedience in the Same Direction*, pg. 16
[5] Lamentations 3:23-24

shocking and very difficult to understand, at least, for me.

> I have been crucified with Christ; it is no longer I who live, but Christ lives in me. **(Galatians 2:20)**
>
> [You] were taught…to put off your old self, which belongs to your former manner of life and is corrupt through deceitful desires, and to be renewed in the spirit of your minds, and to put on the new self, created after the likeness of God in true righteousness and holiness. **(Ephesians 4:22-24 ESV)**
>
> For you died, and your life is hidden with Christ in God. **(Colossians 3:3)**
>
> For as many as are led by the Spirit of God, these are sons of God. **(Romans 8:14)**

As I read these verses, I wondered how to live their truths. At some point, I began to once again struggle with old patterns of thinking and doing. The excitement and newness were beginning to fade as some of the old struggles resurfaced. Somehow, I needed to try to be the new person scripture said I was. Talk about an identity crisis! If I were a new man, why were these old ways returning to me? If I were hidden with Christ in God, why was I sometimes feeling exposed to the hopelessness and emptiness of my previous life? If I were a son of God, why did the opinion of others matter so much?

Is it because these deep truths take time to become our daily reality? It has been my experience that the Holy Spirit has gradually reoriented my soul to the newness of life Jesus purchased for me. And I think Paul would agree. He instructs the churches in Rome,

> ...but be transformed (changed) by the entire renewal of your mind [by its new ideals and its new attitude], so that you may prove what is the good and acceptable and perfect will of God. **(Romans 12:2 AMP)**

And to the church in Corinth:

> And we all, with unveiled face, continually seeing as in a mirror the glory of the Lord, are progressively being transformed into His image from [one degree of] glory to [even more] glory, which comes from the Lord, [who is] the Spirit. **(2 Corinthians 3:18 AMP)**

Under the pressure to be transformed, I began striving to live these truths by my own strength and understanding. This led to frustration and disappointment as I was unable to change myself. As I walk this path with Jesus, He reveals my true identity to me. This, I believe, is the transformative work of the Holy Spirit in my life. Transformation is inevitable as I grow in an understanding of His heart for me, which defines who I am. The transforming power of the gospel is the deepening revelation of his love for me. It has been my experience that it takes time to learn to trust Jesus and to grow into these truths of being a new creation.

Clarifying identity takes time

A revelation came to me recently while on a personal retreat at a Catholic contemplative retreat center. As I sat alone in the woods, immersed in God's stunning creation, my mind began to drift, and I recognized the image of a person deep down in the middle of my being. He was covered in clutter and a tangled web of something I couldn't define. I'm not sure how it was revealed, but I knew that little person was me, the real me. He had been there all along, but was obscured by all the debris in my soul. How in the world could that person possibly emerge from this confused, tangled web? What could I do to help him? I felt helpless. A hand reached down and began to pull this little person through the clutter. There was a nail scar on the hand.

During this brief mystical encounter, I believe it was revealed to me that this was the work of God in my life – my entire life! He was revealing and bringing out the real me who He had known before the foundations of the world were laid. I've been buried beneath so much meaningless clutter. Clutter began to accumulate as soon as I was old enough to gain an understanding of the world in which I was born. This, I knew internally, was the journey I had been on my entire life.

We have several young grandchildren who are growing up quickly. It's fascinating to see their personalities as they emerge. It's also worth realizing that as we observe their personalities, we innately begin to recognize and assess their strengths and weaknesses. As it is clear they are searching for their own identity, the truth is that we are also beginning to do the same. We focus on and build up strengths while trying to address weaknesses. As humans, it is natural and right for us to participate in the development of those entrusted to us. We love and care for them and do play a key role in the development of their identities, for better or worse. I find myself wanting to continually encourage my grandchildren to be patient and allow God to reveal who He created them to be. If only I could consistently live my own advice!

Our culture sends a strong message about the importance of clarifying identity and becoming the people we desire to become. The travesty is that it takes time and life experience to learn these deep truths. Instant satisfaction and obtaining our rightful pleasure now are included in the culture's "claim your identity" package.

The idea of a slowly growing and maturing interior life of God's good revelation of who we are is contrary to almost everything we see and hear daily. It is clear from scripture, however, that God's way is usually slow. Salvation is instantaneous the second we accept Jesus as our Lord and Savior and receive the forgiveness He purchased for our sins. Lasting transformation, however, takes time. It takes time for God to reveal our true selves as He removes the clutter and illusion from our lives. Thomas Merton says:

> The secret of my identity is hidden in the love and mercy of God…Therefore there is only one problem on which all my existence, my peace and my happiness depend: to discover myself in discovering God. If I find Him I will find myself and if I find my true self I will find Him.[6]

This, I believe, is the purpose of the long obedience in the same direction: to find our true selves hidden in Christ as we grow in trust and understanding of His

---

[6] Thomas Merton, *New Seeds of Contemplation* (New York: New Directions Books, 1972), pgs. 35&36

heart for us. Merton refers to "supernatural missions" that God brings to our lives in order to help us grow in the knowledge of who we are. These are opportunities to make choices to trust Him and His promises.

> These missions…take on practical meaning in our lives when we become capable of conscious acts of love. From then on, our life becomes a series of choices between the fiction of our false self, whom we feed with the illusions of passion and selfish appetite, and our loving consent to the purely gratuitous mercy of God.[7]

This is how and what we learn on this long path of obedience as we grow in wisdom and understanding. Our true self is revealed as trust in God's goodness and favor grows over our lifetime. Merton continues,

> When I consent to the will and the mercy of God as it "comes" to me in the events of life, appealing to my inner self and awakening faith, I break through the superficial exterior appearances that form my routine vision of the world and my own self, and I find myself in the presence of hidden majesty.[8]

It seems to me that the revelation of true identity is a primary purpose of discipleship as described in the gospels. By what He taught and how He lived, Jesus was reshaping the identities of His disciples and followers. He was constantly challenging their ideas and understanding of both who He was and who they

---

[7] Thomas Merton, *New Seeds of Contemplation*, pg. 41 (paraphrased)
[8] Ibid, pg. 41

were. Like a sculptor works on a block of marble, Jesus was slowly chipping away at things like narcissism, pragmatism, and restlessness that cluttered and hid their true identities. He was redefining their lives according to His true plan and purposes. This is the long obedience in the same direction Jesus called them to while He walked on the earth, which would continue for the rest of their lives.

Faithful to the end

Jesus also talked to His disciples about the importance of remaining faithful to the end.[9] He was preparing His followers for what lay ahead and encouraging them to stay the course even when things became difficult. In Matthew 10, Jesus is describing sobering truths with His followers about what is to come, especially persecution that would come to believers. He is clear in verse 22 that finishing the work given to us is critical: *But he who endures to the end will be saved.*

Paul also talks about finishing his work in his second letter to Timothy. He's also clear about the rewards of persevering with Jesus,

> I have fought the good fight, I have finished the race, I have kept the faith. Finally, there is laid up for me the crown of righteousness, which the Lord, the righteous Judge, will give to me on that Day, and not to me only but also to all who have loved His appearing. **(2 Timothy 4:7-8)**

---

[9] See for example Mark 13:13; Matthew 10:22

At the end of our lives, we all long to hear the words from the King in the parable of the sheep and goats Jesus uses to describe His judgment of the nations,

> Then the King will say to those on His right hand, 'Come, you blessed of My Father, inherit the kingdom prepared for you from the foundation of the world…' **(Matthew 25:34)**

Jesus spoke of being faithful until the end several times in scripture, so it was obviously an important message to Him. This long obedience in the same direction is what will empower us to remain faithful until the end. It's only as our relationship with Jesus deepens and we can better hear His voice that we will complete the work He has for us. It is clear from His teachings that remaining faithful until the end is not a given. Our growing confidence in His goodness and faithfulness, however, is enough to sustain us.

It's real

> And we know that all things work together for good to those who love God, to those who are the called according to His purpose. For whom He foreknew, He also predestined to be conformed to the image of His Son, that He might be the firstborn among many brethren. **(Romans 8:28-29)**

My youngest was the last to find her soul-mate and commit to the covenant of marriage. As her wedding day approached, I pondered our long journey of raising four kids, wondering how we'd arrived at this significant milestone. I was preparing for the obligatory remarks from the father-of-the-bride at the reception -

this would be my last chance to wow our wedding guests.

I recalled how my life changed that fateful night in Munich, Germany, 35+ years ago, when Jesus introduced Himself to me in a mystical encounter. He invited me on what I'd hoped would be a life-long journey with Him, and I accepted while my head spun and my body trembled. As I looked back at my life from the perspective of my spiritual journey that began that night - all the struggles, failures, and weak attempts at following Him - it was as though a veil was removed from my understanding and I was given a glimpse of His presence with me throughout it all. Overwhelmed by His goodness, I was undone as He revealed it was never about what I could accomplish for Him or how faithful I was. It was always about Him and His immeasurable love for me and faithfulness to me. He had truly been with me the entire time, even when I felt He'd abandoned me because of my weakness and sin. Even through my darkest times of willful sin and self-loathing from the weight of guilt, He was there with me. I had arrived at this point in my life because of the faithfulness of Jesus – period!

Like that night in Munich, this experience while preparing my wedding remarks was another life-changing mystical moment with my loving Savior. His words to the disciples, also a promise to us, are true: *and lo, I am with you always, even to the end of the age.* (Matthew 28:2) My words at the wedding that wonderful April afternoon were few. I had no jokes or funny stories about my daughter. All I could offer was a message of the faithfulness of a loving God. That would have to be enough.

His Constant Call

For almost two-thirds of my life, He and I have walked together. Or, perhaps, it's more appropriate to say He has carried me. So much of the time His presence has either been hidden from me or undiscernible by me. It is likely my attention has mostly been focused somewhere other than on Him. At times, it seemed I'd been hanging on by a single, frayed thread that could break at any moment.

Without fail, however, at moments along the path, and just in time, He pulls back the veil that covers my eyes and reveals His faithfulness and presence in my life. He has always been drawing me to Himself. He has always been patiently helping me understand myself. I breathe and can take another step…He is my forever friend.

Chapter 9

COMMUNITY

For God never makes private, secret salvation deals with people. His relationships with us are personal, true; intimate, yes; but private, no. We are a family in Christ. When we become Christians, we are among brothers and sisters in faith. No Christian is an only child… God never works with individuals in isolation, but always with people in community.[1]

Behold, how good and how pleasant it is for brethren to dwell together in unity! …for there the Lord commanded the blessing—Life forevermore. **(Psalm 133:1&3)**

Walking with others

We have been describing an intimate journey with the Lord that requires much time spent alone with Him. This beautiful, intimate relationship, however, is only one aspect of our dynamic interaction with our Creator. Thomas Merton's words are emphatic:

> There is no true solitude except interior solitude. And interior solitude is not possible

---

[1] Eugene Peterson, *A Long Obedience in the Same Direction* (Downers Grove: InterVarsity Press, 2000) pgs. 175 & 177

> for anyone who does not accept his right place with other men...Solitude is not separation.[2]

The other part of this relationship, equally important if you believe the words of Jesus, regards our lives with others. Consider that Jesus chose His twelve disciples and then commanded them to love one another,

> You did not choose Me, but I chose you and appointed you that you should go and bear fruit, and that your fruit should remain, that whatever you ask the Father in My name He may give you. These things I command you, that you love one another. **(John 15:12-17)**

What an amazing thought! They weren't randomly selected because they were in the right place at the right time. Each from different backgrounds with social, financial, and educational differences called to come together for the common cause of following Jesus. It was in that small community that they learned to live together and love one another according to His plan.

So many of Jesus's teachings are directed at the interactions between His followers and a call for radical reorganization of social structures and relationships. The Sermon on the Mount in Matthew's gospel is a primary example.[3] A main emphasis of Jesus's teaching on this hillside is providing instruction about our relationships with one another. For example, He says,

> Do not judge and criticize and condemn others, so that you may not be judged and criticized

---

[2] Thomas Merton, *New Seeds of Contemplation* (New York: New Directions Books) pg. 56

[3] Matthew 5-7

> and condemned yourselves. For just as you judge and criticize and condemn others you will be judged and criticized and condemned, and in accordance with the measure you deal out to others, it will be dealt out again to you. Why do you stare from without at the very small particle that is in your brother's eye but do not become aware of and consider the beam of timber that is in your own eye? **(Matthew 7:1-3)**

These are astounding words in an honor/shame culture where the gospels imply that men and women were judged continually by their ability to live according to the strict Mosaic law. Their lives were governed by the judgment of the religious leaders, like the Pharisees and Sadducees, who determined how all Israelites were to live under the law. It seems reasonable to assume that, as they lived under continual judgment, they also judged one another as we do. These words present a new way of life, which Jesus described as the Kingdom of God. This was an entirely new way of relating to one another.

All of Paul's pastoral letters to the young churches throughout the Roman Empire addressed the importance of a functioning, loving community. In fact, all of his letters address some sort of conflict within the small communities as they were learning to relate to one another. Many of these church-goers were Roman citizens coming out of polytheism who were now being told there is only one God and all others are false. The new gospel upended all of their beliefs. The Jews in these local communities were also being challenged, as their historic faith had now become something different. Paul worked hard to communicate that Jesus hadn't abolished the ancient law that governed the Israelites, but instead had fulfilled it. But life for Israelite believers was forever changed. Additionally, the Romans didn't like the Jews, and vice versa. This gospel message flew in the face of all the cultural norms of the day as well as the societal structure. In his letter to the church in Corinth, Paul communicates in great detail the heart of our Creator for life together. This was a crucial message that required clear, logical thought.

> For as the body is one and has many members, but all the members of that one body, being many, are one body, so also is Christ. For by one Spirit we were all baptized into one body—whether Jews or Greeks, whether slaves or free—and have all been made to drink into one Spirit. For in fact the body is not one member but many. **(1 Corinthians 12:12-14)**

Paul's first challenge is to dispel any competition between social groups and convince these people that they are all one in Christ. Imagine how difficult this must have been for him to begin breaking down these centuries-old walls of segregation. The work of the Holy Spirit in the midst of these small communities is remarkable. Paul goes on,

> If the foot should say, "Because I am not a hand, I am not of the body," is it therefore not of the body? And if the ear should say, "Because I am not an eye, I am not of the body," is it therefore not of the body? If the whole body were an eye, where would be the hearing? If the whole were hearing, where would be the smelling? But now God has set

> the members, each one of them, in the body just as He pleased. And if they were all one member, where would the body be?
> **(1 Corinthians 12:15-19)**

While emphasizing their equality, he is also sending a message about the importance of their unique individuality. In a culture where individuals are completely defined by social class, race, gender, and citizenship, this message had to have shaken the societal norms.

The final line of this powerful analogy makes Paul's message crystal clear: *Now you are the body of Christ, and members individually.* (1 Corinthians 12:27) They are members of the body of Christ as well as individuals in an intimate relationship with Jesus. Both are crucial and necessary for spiritual growth. Gene Edwards sums up this need to walk together in community nicely:

> So what has been missing? A corporate endeavor! A group of men and women together seeking to know nothing but Christ. This is what has been missing. This, the corporate venture, is what makes the difference…this is what takes away the difficulty. To put it more practically, when a group of people, standing together with one another, seek to live constantly in fellowship with Christ, suddenly the impossible is very obtainable.[4]

---

[4] Gene Edwards, Forward in Brother Lawrence and Frank Laubach, *Practicing His Presence* (Jacksonville: The SeedSowers) pg. vi

His Constant Call

The importance of walking this journey of intimacy with Jesus in community cannot be overstated. Our community is defined not by who we are individually, but by a mystical connection we have in the commonality of commitment to Jesus. What He has done and is doing in each of us defines our lives together. The power of the Holy Spirit working in our midst and empowering us to serve and prefer one another is what a community of believers is all about. Position and anointing are unimportant as true believers embody the life of service Jesus demonstrated.

Dietrich Bonhoeffer powerfully summarizes our need for one another:

> The Christian needs another Christian who speaks God's Word to him. He needs him again and again when he becomes uncertain and discouraged, for by himself he cannot help himself without belying the truth. He needs his brother man as a bearer and proclaimer of the divine word of salvation. He needs his brother solely because of Jesus Christ. The Christ in his own heart is weaker than the Christ in the word of his brother; his own heart is uncertain, his brother's is sure.[5]

Teresa of Avila also had powerful thoughts about the importance of community in the life of the believer.

> For the foundress (Teresa of Avila), growth must happen in the midst of a life lived on a battlefield. The man or woman who aspires

---

[5] Dietrich Bonhoeffer, quoted in Eugene Peterson, *A Long Obedience in the Same Direction*, pg. 181

> to lofty contemplation ordinarily lives in a community of one kind or another, with all its demands for kindness, patience, humility, forgiveness, and obedience. One does not satisfy conditions for prayer "by getting alone in corners."[6]

We can only grow in grace if we learn to live together in unity. While this journey is individual and intimate, there is also a need for human fellowship and companionship that our Creator has hard-wired into each human being.

Church community

> As iron sharpens iron, so a man sharpens the countenance of his friend. **(Proverbs 27:17)**

The idea of "church" has been defined and redefined for centuries. The word, first used by Jesus[7], comes from the Greek *ekklēsia,* which means: an assembly or religious congregation. Scripture is conspicuously (and frustratingly) nebulous about how to "do" church or how to operate this community of believers. There is some guidance, from Paul especially, regarding roles and responsibilities, but scripture does not contain a "how-to" manual when it comes to operating a church. Scripture is clear, however, that there is only one church on earth, and Jesus is the head. Paul writes to the church in Colossae:

---

[6] Thomas Dubay, *Fire Within* (San Francisco: Ignatius Press, 1989) pg. 128
[7] Matthew 16:18

> And He is the head of the body, the church, who is the beginning, the firstborn from the dead, that in all things He may have the preeminence. **(Colossians 1:18)**

However church is defined or operated, it is clear that Jesus is in charge and all our human formats and structures will one day be dissolved as the Spirit brings us together in unity before our Lord. The Bible tells us that one day, we will be presented together as a spotless bride to our Savior husband.[8]

Together, our church community has walked this path of first establishing a regular prayer life and then learning the practice of contemplative prayer. We've stumbled, fallen, and stubbed our toes while finding our footing on this life-changing path, but we have persevered for almost a quarter of a century.

The following is a summary of our church community's journey towards learning to live the contemplative life. My intention is not to propose a church structure or suggest our community as the best model. It's simply to share our experience.

Take responsibility

One of the most important messages taught by our leadership from the beginning was that we are individually responsible for our relationship with God. We agreed to be "committed to take Jesus at least as seriously as everything else in our lives." Our leaders have had pastoral and other giftings, Paul describes in Ephesians 4:11, given with a purpose:

---

[8] Revelation 19:8

> ...to fully equip and perfect the saints (God's people) for works of service, to build up the body of Christ [the church]; **(Ephesians 4:12 AMP)**

My leaders are not responsible, however, for my relationship with Jesus – I'm primarily accountable for that. Yes, they lead, encourage, rebuke, assist, and instruct, but only for those who willingly assume responsibility for this relationship with our Savior. An emphasis was also placed on how our individual relationships with the Lord impact the spiritual health of the community. This was a powerful transition from the church model that requires leaders to shoulder this burden themselves. We (members) share responsibility and are called to a higher standard to minister to one another. I believe Paul speaks of this in his letter to the church in Ephesus,

> ... that we should no longer be children, tossed to and fro and carried about with every wind of doctrine...but, speaking the truth in love, may grow up in all things into Him who is the head—Christ— from whom the whole body, joined and knit together by what every joint supplies, according to the effective working by which every part does its share, causes growth of the body for the edifying of itself in love. **(Ephesians 4:14-16)**

Our gatherings are times of worship and celebration, and we are expected to come prepared to give, as well as to receive. This responsibility was important as we established our own prayer lives. There were many mornings I was motivated to spend time with Jesus because of the nagging sense of responsibility to others

His Constant Call

in our church body. If they were committed, I needed to be committed too. We were on this journey together. It wasn't the commitment to prayer that impacted the spiritual health of the church; it was the transformational work of the Holy Spirit during prayer that positively affected our community. The unity of the body was dependent upon our deepening individual relationships with Jesus.

Our pastor's messages were instructional, encouraging, and lovingly demanding as together we learned what a life committed to prayer and, specifically, contemplative prayer, looked like. We had church retreats and adult getaways focused on contemplative prayer. These were opportunities to practice what we were learning about prayer as well as to encourage one another. Weekly meetings like small groups, book groups, or other teaching services all started with 5-10 minutes of silence. These times provided us with the opportunity as a community of believers to practice quieting our hearts and minds in preparation for receiving what the Lord had for us.

The church doors were opened every Sunday at least an hour before service with soft, instrumental music playing to create a quiet atmosphere for prayer. Church members who volunteer to minister to those who come forward for prayer were required to come to church an hour early and prepare their hearts for service. These activities continue to this day.

One of the most powerful and enduring activities implemented by our leadership many years ago was, and is still, an opportunity for members to share the impact of contemplative prayer in their lives. One Sunday per month, three or four individuals volunteer to share how God is speaking to them in the circumstances of their lives. These are powerful testimonials of the depth at which the Holy Spirit works in His children. The honesty, vulnerability, transparency, and humility of these members encourage our entire body that we are not alone in our struggles to be transformed into the image of Christ. We are all aware of our enemy's strategy of isolating us and whispering that "no one understands my struggle," or "my sin is too great for the power of the cross." Sharing our struggles in an appropriate but honest way defuses the impact and power of these lies. Additionally, those who speak come to realize the weight of sharing before their brothers and sisters. This includes learning to listen for and discern what the Lord is doing and saying to us. We are then confronted with the challenge of finding words to express His work in our lives.

We've not walked perfectly, and I'm not presenting our body as a model community. We have, however, experienced a depth of honesty and transparency in our relationships that I believe is the fruit of the contemplative life.

Chapter 10

GROWING IN COMPASSION

He has told you, O man, what is good; and what does the Lord require of you except to be just, and to love [and to diligently practice] kindness (compassion), and to walk humbly with your God [setting aside any overblown sense of importance or self-righteousness]? **(Micah 6:8 AMP)**

Serious and humble prayer, united with mature love, will unconsciously and spontaneously manifest itself in a habitual spirit of sacrifice and concern for others that is unfailingly generous, though perhaps we may not be aware of the fact.[1]

Our challenge

Up to this point, I have attempted to describe contemplative prayer and how this intimate relationship with the Holy Trinity impacts our lives, both individually and within a community of believers. The work of the Holy Spirit in our lives through contemplative prayer opens our eyes, ears, and hearts to the glory and splendor of our Creator all around us. This means that our spirits should become better in tune with God's

---

[1] Thomas Merton, *Contemplative Prayer* (New York: Random House LLC, 1996) pg. 52

heart and mind, and this includes His love and concern for all of humanity. The impact of contemplative prayer in our lives leads to greater compassion and love for not only our brothers and sisters in Christ, but also the lost who have not yet opened the door of their hearts to our Savior. In other words, contemplative prayer leads to some kind of action and greater charity[2] in our lives as we are compelled to share the life we are receiving. I'm referring to being motivated by a charitable heart of love towards our neighbors, including those in need. If we are not growing in love for others, which then motivates our actions, we are missing the intent of the Kingdom of God.

Dangerously free

Father Richard Rohr, a modern-day contemplative and founder of the Center for Action and Contemplation, provides a powerful summary in his August 22, 2022, Daily Meditation:

> I'm convinced that if we stick with it, if we practice contemplation regularly, then we will come to an inner place of compassion—for ourselves and for others. In this place, we notice how much the suffering of the world is our suffering. We become committed to this world, not cerebrally, but from the much deeper perspective of our soul. At this point, we're indestructible, because in that place we find the peace that the world cannot give. We

---

[2] Charity - generosity and helpfulness especially toward the needy or suffering; benevolent goodwill toward or love of humanity; (Merriam-Webster Dictionary)

> don't need to win anymore; we just need to do what we have to do, as naive and simplistic as that might sound. That's why Augustine could make such an outrageous statement as "Love [God] and do what you will"! People who are living from a truly God-centered place instead of a self-centered place are dangerously free precisely because they are tethered at the center.[3]

If our hearts are not being transformed to carry more compassion for those in need and pain around us, we are either resisting the work of God in our lives or have become dull to the Holy Spirit. As children of our good Father, His life in us will increase so we can be "dangerously free" to serve. Thomas Merton adds,

> One of the paradoxes of the mystical life is this: that a man cannot enter into the deepest center of himself and pass through that center into God, unless he is able to pass entirely out of himself to other people in the purity of a selfless love.[4]

Those at the heart of God

We've already discussed life together on this journey as a community of believers. Let's now look at the people who seem to be at the heart of God throughout the Bible.

---

[3] Richard Rohr Daily Meditation, Monday, August 22, 2022. Week Thirty-Four: Discerning What is Ours to Do

[4] Thomas Merton, *New Seeds of Contemplation* (New York: New Directions Books, 2007) pg. 64

My intention is not to define the Kingdom of God in detail or to describe the life I believe we are called to live. We must all determine how God is calling us to lead our lives and follow the guidance of the Holy Spirit. It seems to me, however, that throughout the Bible, and culminating in the actions and words of Jesus, there are people God has instructed us to be aware of, serve, and help. Beginning in Exodus and throughout the Old Testament, Yahweh makes His heart known to the vulnerable individuals of society.

The following are just a few scriptures, beginning with the Old Testament, that seem to send a clear message of those vulnerable groups in society who are at the heart of the Father: widows, orphans, the poor, and immigrants. These are presented for your own meditation.

> You shall neither mistreat a stranger nor oppress him, for you were strangers in the land of Egypt. You shall not afflict any widow or fatherless child. If you afflict them in any way, and they cry at all to Me, I will surely hear their cry; and My wrath will become hot, and I will kill you with the sword; your wives shall be widows, and your children fatherless. If you lend money to any of My people who are poor among you, you shall not be like a moneylender to him; you shall not charge him interest. **(Exodus 22:21-25)**

> And if a stranger dwells with you in your land, you shall not mistreat him. The stranger who dwells among you shall be to you as one born among you, and you shall love him as yourself;

for you were strangers in the land of Egypt: I am the Lord your God. **(Leviticus 19:33-34)**

He administers justice for the fatherless and the widow, and loves the stranger, giving him food and clothing. Therefore love the stranger, for you were strangers in the land of Egypt. **(Deuteronomy 10:18-19)**

A father of the fatherless, a defender of widows, Is God in His holy habitation. God sets the solitary in families; He brings out those who are bound into prosperity; but the rebellious dwell in a dry land. **(Psalm 68:5-6)**

The helpless commits himself to You; You are the helper of the fatherless. **(Psalm 10:14)**

He who oppresses the poor reproaches his Maker, but he who honors Him has mercy on the needy. **(Proverbs 14:31)**

Thus says the Lord: "Execute judgment and righteousness, and deliver the plundered out of the hand of the oppressor. Do no wrong and do no violence to the stranger, the fatherless, or the widow, nor shed innocent blood in this place. **(Jeremiah 22:3)**

For in You the fatherless finds mercy. **(Hosea 14:3)**

Jesus reiterated the same messages from the Old Testament through His actions and words. Additionally, He said many surprising and difficult things for our Western ears to hear regarding the use of money and God's provision, and the treatment of others. The

His Constant Call

following are just a few of those statements from the gospels.

> Then one of them, a lawyer, asked Him a question, testing Him, and saying, "Teacher, which is the great commandment in the law?" Jesus said to him, "'You shall love the Lord your God with all your heart, with all your soul, and with all your mind.' This is the first and great commandment. And the second is like it: 'You shall love your neighbor (others) as yourself.' On these two commandments hang all the Law and the Prophets." **(Matthew 22:35-40)**
>
> But God said to him, 'You fool! This very night your soul is required of you; and now who will own all the things you have prepared?' So it is for the one who continues to store up and hoard possessions for himself, and is not rich [in his relationship] toward God. **(Luke 12:20-21 AMP)**
>
> Sell your possessions (show compassion) and give [donations] to the poor. Provide money belts for yourselves that do not wear out, an unfailing and inexhaustible treasure in the heavens, where no thief comes near and no moth destroys. For where your treasure is, there your heart will be also. **(Luke 12:33-34 AMP)**
>
> Then he said to his servants, 'The wedding [feast]is ready, but those who were invited were not worthy. So go to the main highways that lead out of the city, and invite to the wedding

> feast as many as you find.' Those servants went out into the streets and gathered together all the people they could find, both bad and good; so the wedding hall was filled with dinner guests [sitting at the banquet table]. **(Matthew 22:8-10 AMP)**
>
> But when you give a feast, invite the poor, the maimed, the lame, the blind. **(Luke 14:13)**

Father Rolheiser's words in *The Shattered Lantern* are poignant,

> We know that our faith calls us to work for social justice and that this demand is non-negotiable. We know too, as somebody once put it with a succinctness that is praiseworthy, that strength without compassion is violence; that compassion without justice is weakness; that justice without love is Marxism; and that love without justice is baloney![5]

He goes on:

> The hardest thing to sustain within our lives today is prayer. Everything militates against it. Given this, perhaps the only way we have of not letting ourselves be swallowed whole by our culture is to kiss the leper, to place our lot with those who have no place within the culture, namely, the poor with their many faces: the aged, the sick, the dying, the unborn, the handicapped, the unattractive, the displaced,

---

[5] Ronald Rolheiser, *The Shattered Lantern* (New York: The Crossroad Publishing Company, 2001) pg. 201

> and all those others that are not valued by our culture. To touch those who have no place within our culture is to give ourselves a perspective beyond our culture.[6]

And here is where the rubber meets the road in our lives. As I look back at my life, He has demonstrated over and over again that He is faithful and trustworthy in ALL things. And yet, the desire to live a more surrendered life sometimes seems unattainable. The reason has to be that there is still doubt and unbelief in my soul. It's more than simply living our lives before Him. There must be intention in the things we do and the way we both hold and open our hearts and lives to others.

We must be careful, however, not to define 'action' based on someone else's definition. We tend to minimize and be quick to disregard the daily responsibilities of our 'mundane' lives instead of recognizing opportunities He presents to us in the midst of them. Jesus is our example; a deepening revelation of His heart, His heart for us, and obedience to His leading are critical. Henri Nouwen's words are powerful:

> This purity of heart allows us to see more clearly, not only our own needy, distorted, and anxious self but also the caring face of our compassionate God. When that vision remains clear and sharp, it will be possible to move into the midst of a tumultuous world with a heart at rest. It is this restful heart that will attract those

---

[6] Ronald Rolheiser, *The Shattered Lantern*, pgs. 201-202

> who are groping to find their way through life. When we have found rest in God, we can do nothing other than minister.[7]

The poignant words of Jesus as he spoke at length to His disciples from Matthew's Gospel seemed a good place to end this chapter. He did not mince words regarding expectations of how His disciples should treat other people.

> When the Son of Man comes in His glory, and all the holy angels with Him, then He will sit on the throne of His glory. All the nations will be gathered before Him, and He will separate them one from another, as a shepherd divides his sheep from the goats. And He will set the sheep on His right hand, but the goats on the left. Then the King will say to those on His right hand, 'Come, you blessed of My Father, inherit the kingdom prepared for you from the foundation of the world: for I was hungry and you gave Me food; I was thirsty and you gave Me drink; I was a stranger and you took Me in; I was naked and you clothed Me; I was sick and you visited Me; I was in prison and you came to Me.'

> Then the righteous will answer Him, saying, 'Lord, when did we see You hungry and feed You, or thirsty and give You drink? When did we see You a stranger and take You in, or naked and clothe You? Or when did we see You sick,

---

[7] Henri Nouwen, *The Way of the Heart* (New York: Ballantine Books, 1981), pg. 90

or in prison, and come to You?' And the King will answer and say to them, 'Assuredly, I say to you, inasmuch as you did it to one of the least of these My brethren, you did it to Me.'

Then He will also say to those on the left hand, 'Depart from Me, you cursed, into the everlasting fire prepared for the devil and his angels: for I was hungry and you gave Me no food; I was thirsty and you gave Me no drink; I was a stranger and you did not take Me in, naked and you did not clothe Me, sick and in prison and you did not visit Me.'

Then they also will answer Him, saying, 'Lord, when did we see You hungry or thirsty or a stranger or naked or sick or in prison, and did not minister to You?' Then He will answer them, saying, 'Assuredly, I say to you, inasmuch as you did not do it to one of the least of these, you did not do it to Me.' And these will go away into everlasting punishment, but the righteous into eternal life. **(Matthew 25: 31-46)**

Epilogue

"For all these things My hand has made, so all these things came into being [by and for Me]," declares the Lord. "But to this one I will look [graciously], to him who is humble and contrite in spirit, and who [reverently] trembles at My word and honors My commands." **(Isaiah 66:2 AMP)**

If you're still reading, I'd like to think that my words have had some kind of impact on you. As I conclude this primer, I believe it's worth reiterating the staggering truth of the relentless pursuit of our Holy God to be with His created people. From cover to cover, the Bible tells this story in beautiful detail. The final and complete fulfillment of His heart's desire was to make a permanent way to be together through the death, resurrection, and ascension of His Son, Jesus. His heart has always desired to be loved by humans who choose Him of their own free will. He woos and draws us constantly, but will never violate our free will and individual choice to respond to His call and bend our knees to Him as Lord.

Our pursuit of Him and the required discipline should not be viewed as a chore or burden we must bear in order to receive His blessings. In my self-centeredness and arrogance, I have often defaulted to this delusional posture of self-pity and self-sacrifice. **The truth is that the biblical story is about invitation**. We have all been invited into a relationship with the Creator of the

Cosmos, who desires to spend time with us. Let this truth hit and sink in. Responding to this invitation is simply to say "yes" to His call; to let Him into your life. It is by responding to this invitation that we are changed and renewed through His incomparable kindness and goodness. He is gracious and patient as we allow Him into the depths of our hearts and souls, where the real healing and transformation needs to take place. As we learn to walk with Him and simply be with Him, we will daily find opportunities to trust Him and know that He can be trusted. **This is the secret to a life of peace and happiness – trusting in God's heart for us**!

The spiritual life is full of paradox. For example, we are told to pray for all things (Matthew 7:7-8) to a God who knows what we will pray for before we even ask (Matthew 6:8). Why? I believe it's because He desires to interact with us individually. There are many mysteries of the spiritual journey we will not understand during this lifetime. For example, we will never be able to eliminate the tension inherent in a love relationship between the Creator and the created (us). Our human minds have no context for this type of relationship and the mystery it is enshrouded in.

In his book, *Ruthless Trust: The Ragamuffin's Path to God*, pastor and author Brennan Manning's words sum up our primary struggle living within the mysteries of God: 'And mystery is an embarrassment to the modern human mind.'[1] How true! My mind often reels in frustration at my lack of understanding about spiritual

---

[1] Brennan Manning, *Ruthless Trust: The Ragamuffin's Path to God* (New York: HarperOne, 2000) pg. 57

things. We must recognize, however, that while on this earth, this relationship is based on faith. Complete understanding is simply not possible, so we choose to believe. Further, I agree with Manning that our faith needs to be accompanied by experience,

> It is simply not possible to receive the revelation of God in the transcendent/immanent Christ without experience. Experience is an essential part of knowing Jesus and of the whole concept of revelation. [2]

If you are lacking experience of His love, ask Him for it.

As we grow in our knowledge of Him, we are also known by Him. Of course, He is omniscient and knows all things, including our hearts, but one of the great mysteries of this amazing relationship is the power of being known by Him. I believe it is critically important that we know He knows us intimately. He knows the real me and still chooses me. His love does not grow as we grow. While He is relentless in His purpose to complete His work of transformation in me so that I can love Him more, His love never changes. There truly is no limit to His love, kindness, and faithfulness.

God's promise to His chosen people, Israel, through the Prophet Isaiah rings as true for us today as His adopted children as it did for them thousands of years ago,

---

[2] Brennan Manning, *Ruthless Trust: The Ragamuffin's Path to God*, pgs. 87-88

> 'Do not fear [anything], for I am with you; Do not be afraid, for I am your God. I will strengthen you, be assured I will help you; I will certainly take hold of you with My righteous right hand [a hand of justice, of power, of victory, of salvation].' **(Isaiah 41:10 AMP)**

We need only to keep walking with Him and responding to *His constant call*.

References

Avila, S. T. (2007). *Interior Castle*. Mineola: Dover Publications, Inc.

Barton, R. H. (2018). *Invitation to Retreat*. Downers Grove: Intervarsity Press.

Bickle, M. (2007). *The Song of Songs*. Kansas City: Forerunner Publishing.

Chambers, O. (1992). *My Utmost for His Highest, Updated Edition*. Grand Rapids: Our Daily Bread Publishing.

Chittister, J. (2000). *Illuminated Life*. Maryknoll: Orbis Books.

Comer, J. M. (2019). *The Ruthless Elimination of Hurry*. Coloraod Springs: Waterbrook.

Cross, J. o. (2017). *The Living Flame of Love*. London: Society for Promoting Christian Knowledge.

Cross, S. J. (2003). *Dark Night of the Soul*. Mineola: Dover Publications.

Cross, S. J. (2016). *Ascent of Mount Carmel*. Eastford: Martino Fine Books.

Crowder, J. (2016). *Mystical Union*. Marylhurst: Sons of Thunder Ministries.

Foster, R. (1998). *Celebration of Discipline*. San Francisco: HarperCollins.

Galloway, J. (1990). Contemplation - A Treatise on Mysticism. *Carmelite Digest, Volume 5, Number 4*.

Guyon, J. (1975). *Experiencing the Depths of Jesus Christ*. Jacksonville: SeedSowers Publishing.

Guyon, J. (1984). *Experiencing God Through Prayer*. New Kensington: Whitaker House.

Guyon, J. (1999). *Union With God*. Jacksonville: SeedSowers Publishing.

Halter, H. (2011). *Sacrilege*. Grand Rapids: Baker Books.

Laubach, B. L. (1973). *Practicing His Presence*. Jacksonville: The SeedSowers.

Laubach, F. C. (2007). *Letters by a Modern Mystic*. Colorado Springs: Purposeful Design Publications.

Manning, B. (2000). *Ruthless Trust: The Ragamuffin's Path to God*. New York: HarperOne.

Merton, T. (2007). *New Seed of Contemplation*. New York: New Directions Books.

Merton, T. (2014). *Contemplative Prayer*. New York: Random House.

Miller, C. (1984). *The Table of Inwardness*. Downers Grove: Inter-Varisty Press.

Morales, M. (2015). *Who Shall Ascend the Mountain of the Lord?* Downers Grove: Intervarsity Press.

Nouwen, H. (1981). *Making All Things New: An Invitation to the Spiritual Life*. New York: Doubleday.

Nouwen, H. (1981). *The Way of the Heart*. New York: Ballantine Books.

Peterson, E. H. (2000). *A Long Obedience in the Same Direction*. Downers Grove: InterVarsity Press.

Rolheiser, R. (2001). *The Shattered Lantern*. New York: Crossroad Publishing Co.

Sorge, B. (2018). *Secrets of the Secret Place*. Grandview: Oasis House.

Thomas Dubay, S. (1989). *Fire Within*. San Francisco: Ignatius Press.

Thomas Dubay, S. (1999). *The Evidential Power of Beauty*. San Franscisco: Ignatius Press.

Tozer, A. (1961). *Knowledge of the Holy*. New York: HarperOne.

Unknown. (1973). *The Cloud of Unknowing*. New York: Random House.

Willard, D. (2012). *Hearing God*. Downers Grove: Intervarsity Press.

About Kharis Publishing:

Kharis Publishing, an imprint of Kharis Media LLC, is a leading Christian and inspirational book publisher based in Aurora, Chicago metropolitan area, Illinois. Kharis' dual mission is to give voice to under-represented writers (including women and first-time authors) and equip orphans in developing countries with literacy tools. That is why, for each book sold, the publisher channels some of the proceeds into providing books and computers for orphanages in developing countries so that these kids may learn to read, dream, and grow. For a limited time, Kharis Publishing is accepting unsolicited queries for nonfiction (Christian, self-help, memoirs, business, health and wellness) from qualified leaders, professionals, pastors, and ministers. Learn more at: https://kharispublishing.com/

www.ingramcontent.com/pod-product-compliance
Lightning Source LLC
Chambersburg PA
CBHW060353110426
42743CB00036B/2903